OSPREY AIRCRAFT OF THE A

Israeli Mirage and Nesher Aces

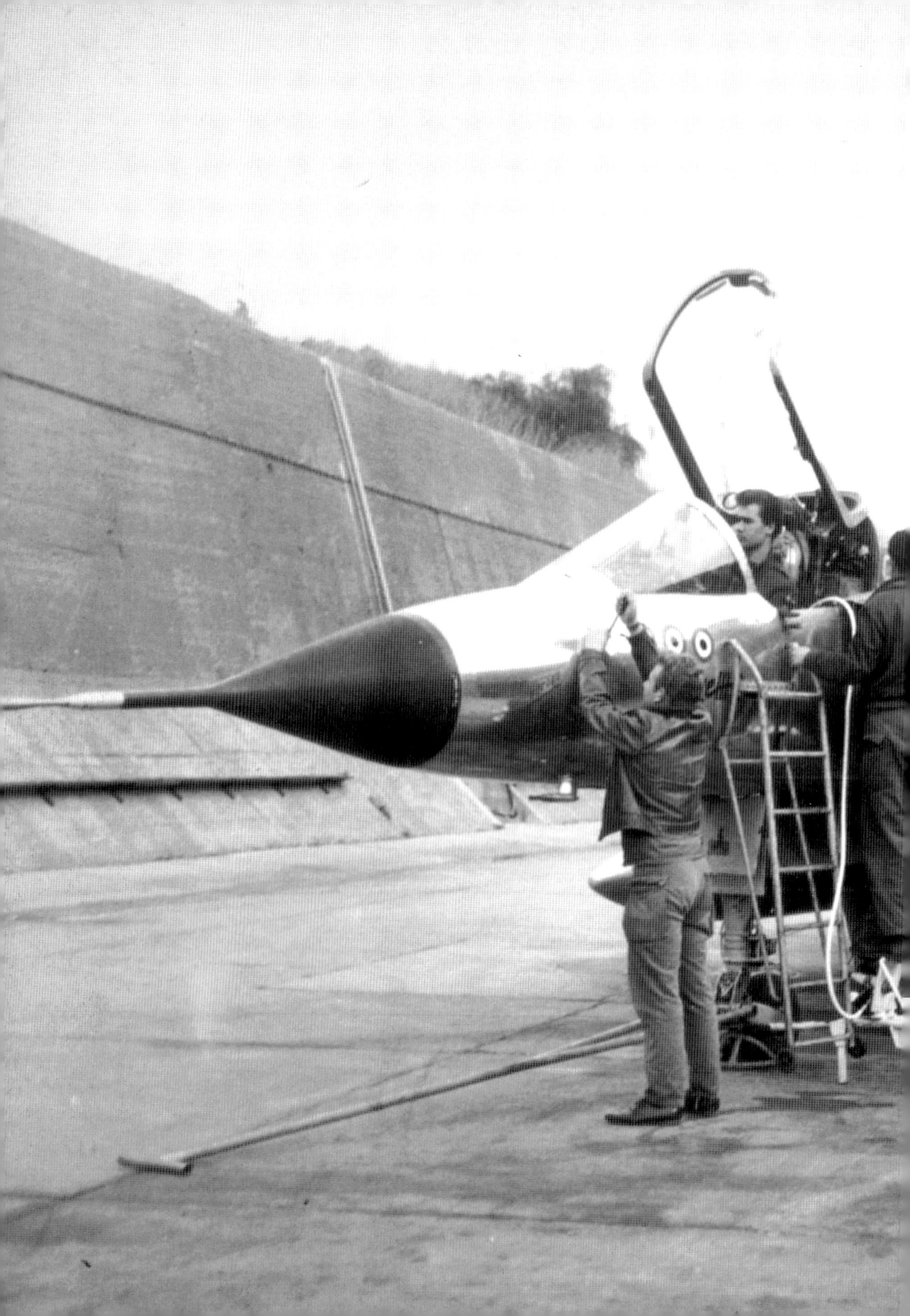

SERIES EDITOR: TONY HOLMES
OSPREY AIRCRAFT OF THE ACES® • 59

Israeli Mirage and Nesher Aces

Shlomo Aloni

OSPREY
PUBLISHING

Front Cover

On the evening of 17 October 1973, six fighter pilots arrived at Refidim, in Sinai, to take over responsibility for keeping a force of Nesher fighters on alert at the forward air base. Avraham Salmon, Dror Harish and Gidon Livni were from No 101 Sqn, while Moshe Hertz, Gidon Dror and Ra'anan Yosef were No 113 Sqn pilots. Hertz was the latter unit's senior deputy CO, while Livni was No 101's reconnaissance officer. Yosef was a No 113 Sqn EP (emergency posting) pilot, and Salmon, Harish and Dror were reserve pilots. All seasoned veterans they already boasted a combined score of 22.5 kills. Salmon and Harish were aces, Dror, Hertz and Livni were on their way and young Yosef would probably have joined this elite 'club' had he been in combat longer.

On 18 October the detachment was active as usual, with Salmon and Dror intercepting Egyptian MiG-17s at noon. Dror reported;

'We arrived over the bridgehead before the attackers. We turned 360 degrees and then saw a four-ship formation of MiG-17s diving from south to north towards the bridges. Avrahamik chased the left-hand MiG but I saw another four-ship formation trailing behind the first. I manoeuvred behind the trailing one, so there were nine aircraft ahead of me – two MiG-17 four-ship formations and Avrahamik in between. I chased the right-hand MiG in the trailing formation and shot it down with a Shafrir 2. Within moments I had shot down the right-hand MiG of the leading formation with my second missile. I manoeuvred behind the remaining three MiGs of the trailing formation. My intention was to use my cannon to shoot down as many as possible. Then Avrahamik called for help. Due to the explosion of the second MiG that I had shot down, his canopy was covered with debris and he could barely see anything. I led him back to a safe landing at Refidim. Six MiGs also returned home safely.'

The alert Neshers at Refidim were in action again in the afternoon, protecting the Israeli bridgehead from Egyptian air strikes. In a multi-bogey engagement, Hertz and Livni, with Harish and Yosef, shot down two MiG-17s and five MiG-21s. Two of the kills were among the most spectacular ever captured by the delta-fighter's gunsight cameras. Flying Nesher 09, Gidon Livni downed a MiG-21 crossing from left to right, while Nesher 10, flown by Ra'anan Yosef, shot down a MiG-21, the gun-sight camera catching it with its braking 'chute deployed – the subject of this cover artwork.

'The attacking MiG-17s and escorting MiG-21s arrived as an armada', Yosef later reported. 'I immediately followed a pair of MiG-21s flying in close formation. One "stitch" and I was behind the trailing MiG. I opened fire and hit the empennage. The MiG lost control, its braking 'chute was deployed, and when it was nearly vertical, pointing downwards, the pilot ejected' (*Cover artwork by Mark Postlethwaite*)

Dedication

This work is dedicated to Nili, Tal, Yael and Maya

First published in Great Britain in 2004 by Osprey Publishing, Midland House, West Way, Botley, Oxford OX2 0PH, UK
443 Park Avenue South, New York, NY 10016, USA
© 2004 Osprey Publishing Limited

All rights reserved. Apart from any fair dealing for the purpose of private study, research, criticism or review, as permitted under the Copyright, Design and Patents Act 1988, no part of this publication may be reproduced, stored in a retrieval system, or transmitted in any form or by any means, electronic, electrical, chemical, mechanical, optical, photocopying, recording or otherwise without prior written permission. All enquiries should be addressed to Osprey.

ISBN 1 84176 653 4

Edited by Tony Holmes and Bruce Hales-Dutton
Page design by Mark Holt
Cover Artwork by Mark Postlethwaite
Aircraft Profiles and Scale Drawings by Mark Styling
Index by Alan Thatcher
Origination by PPS Grasmere Ltd. Leeds, UK
Printed in China through bookbuilders

05 06 07 08   10 9 8 7 6 5 4 3 2

ACKNOWLEDGEMENTS

The author wishes to express his gratitude to the many delta-fighter pilots, friends and colleagues who contributed to the production of this volume. Most of the photos originated from personal collections. More often than not, the same one came from several sources, so to avoid hurting anyone's feelings the author wishes to thank all contributors together, pilots and friends. To save space, as well as to avoid confusion and repetitiveness, no ranks are mentioned in the text except for senior officers such as the IDF/AF CO.

For details of all Osprey Publishing titles please contact us at:
NORTH AMERICA
Osprey Direct, 2427 Bond Street, University Park, IL 60466, USA
E-mail: info@ospreydirectusa.com
ALL OTHER REGIONS
Osprey Direct UK, P.O. Box 140, Wellingborough, Northants, NN8 2FA, UK
E-mail: info@ospreydirect.co.uk
Or visit our website: **www.ospreypublishing.com**

CONTENTS

CHAPTER ONE
MACH ONE AIR WARFARE 6

CHAPTER TWO
SIX DAY WAR 33

CHAPTER THREE
ATTRITION 44

CHAPTER FOUR
THE SOVIETS INTERVENE 57

CHAPTER FIVE
YOM KIPPUR WAR 66

EPILOGUE 79

APPENDICES 81
COLOUR PLATES COMMENTARY 89
INDEX 96

CHAPTER ONE
MACH 2 AIR WARFARE

If results achieved in air-to-air combat are the leading criterion, then the French Dassault Mirage III family probably ranks top among the first generation of Mach 2 fighters. It was one of ten such types flown for the first time from 1954 by the five nations which were capable of producing such technologically advanced military hardware – France, Sweden, UK, USA and USSR.

Under the circumstances, the French achievement is of special interest because the Mirage was not actually the most capable fighter of its kind. Moreover, it was not the first Mach 2 fighter to fly, nor was it the first to enter operational service. And from a technological standpoint, the Mirage III was not as innovative as competitors like the F-104 Starfighter with its thin wing, the F-106 Delta Dart, which preceded the Mirage, the MiG-21, which combined a delta wing with a horizontal stabiliser, the Saab 35 Draken, with its double delta wing, and the English Electric Lightning, with its highly swept wing and unique engine installation.

The Mirage III family did not incorporate breathtaking technology either. The SNECMA Atar 9B-3 turbojet was less powerful than equivalent US powerplants, while the advanced weapon system concept introduced by US fighters was years ahead of anything in the Mirage. Nevertheless, the French fighter was certainly a sales success, although fewer were produced than the MiG-21, the F-104 or the F-4 Phantom II.

Even more amazing is the fact that most of the Mirage's air-to-air kills were claimed by a single customer – an air force which operated less than ten per cent of Mirage III family production. In fact it was the overwhelming operational success of the Israeli Defence Force/Air Force (IDF/AF) which boosted the French delta fighter's commercial success. Export sales more than doubled after the astonishing achievements of IDF/AF Mirages during the Six Day War of June 1967.

Mirage III acquisition was an inevitable development in IDF/AF history. Following Israel's purchase of Dassault's Ouragan in 1955, the Mystere in 1956 and the Super Mystere in 1958, the close links between France and Israel made procurement of the Mirage III a logical consequence. Israel signed its first Mirage IIIC purchase contract in May 1960, and this covered the supply of 24 aircraft, with an option on a further 36. A second contract covering another 24 Mirage IIICs was signed in April 1961, and this was followed by a third, also for 24 Mirage IIICs. Delivery of three Mirage IIIB two-seaters in 1966 and a fourth in 1968 brought the total Israeli purchase to 76.

Although the acquisition of the Mirage came as no great surprise in light of the special diplomatic relationship between France and Israel at that time, the IDF/AF's insistence that the Mirage III interceptor should be turned into a fighter-bomber was controversial. Like most first generation

IDF/AF chief test pilot Danny Shapira (left) was the first Israeli to fly a Mirage III. In June 1959 he demonstrated the new Mach 2 wonder to IDF/AF commander in chief, Maj Gen Ezer Weizman (right). Shapira became only the 12th pilot to achieve Mach 2 in Mirage IIIA03 during the course of the demonstration flight

In order to turn the Mirage III interceptor into the Shahak multi-role combat aircraft, the Israelis focused primarily on the aircraft's ability to carry and deliver bombs. The sleek fuel tanks flanking the bombs were Israeli-developed 500-litre supersonic tanks. Producing less drag than the customary 625-litre subsonic ones, they offered similar endurance/range performance for less weight

Nos 101 and 117 Sqns were declared operational with the R.530 Yahalom AAM between April and July 1964. The initial Israeli weapons purchase from Dassault consisted of just eight pylons, 15 AAMs and three training rounds

Mach 2 fighters, the Mirage III was developed as a point-defence interceptor to counter high-flying bombers carrying nuclear weapons.

To achieve a successful interception as far away as possible from the bomber's target, the fighter had to take-off, day or night in all weather conditions, accelerate and climb extremely fast, while being vectored towards its target by ground control to achieve the best and fastest interception solution. Once the target had been acquired by the onboard weapon system, interception was intended to be an automatic procedure. The fighter was to launch a relatively large air-to-air missile from the longest possible range to ensure the bomber's destruction with, hopefully, no damage to the interceptor. Manoeuvrability, endurance and payload were all sacrificed to produce the ultimate interceptor. Even cannon were discarded because it was assumed that no pilot would be brave enough to close in and shoot down a bomber carrying nuclear weapons.

Maj Gen Ezer Weizman commanded the IDF/AF between 1958 and 1966. He realised that point-defence interceptors were not relevant to Middle East air warfare, and that Israel needed tactical fighter-bombers. Weizman resented the high-low mix imposed upon so many air forces by accountants and economists. He also wanted the best for his pilots, but he did not want to buy a small number of 'high-tech', high price interceptors, thus forcing him to send most of his pilots into battle in obsolete attack aircraft that would be easy prey for the enemy. Ideally, a single type of advanced fighter-bomber could fulfil all IDF/AF mission requirements. It made no sense to despatch a large number of obsolete attack aircraft, escorted by a small number of interceptors, on dangerous missions. But if the attacking force comprised superior fighter-bombers, no escorting interceptors would be needed. A versatile fighter-bomber would be able to attack the target and defend itself against enemy interceptors.

Although such a dream might have seemed impossible, Weizman emerged victorious from the debate with IDF staff and government accountants and economists. Granted, his request for 100 Mirages was never fulfilled, but the purchase of three squadrons of multi-role delta jets was significantly more than the initial intention of acquiring a single squadron of interceptors.

CHAPTER ONE

Factory-fresh Mirage IIICJs are seen ready for delivery to Israel in the early 1960s. Ferry flights between 1962 and 1964 were coded Operation *Zola 1* to *15*, and Danny Shapira participated in all of them. Additionally, he flew four Mirage IIIBJs from France to Israel in 1966-68, bringing to 19 the total number of jets he had personally ferried – exactly a quarter of the total supplied to Israel

Shahak 53 'landed' after Ran Ronen was forced to eject when the engine cut as he was returning from an operational mission in November 1963. The aircraft was not badly damaged, and the failure in the Atar's accessory box was quickly located and repaired

Israeli Mirages dispensed with the SEPR 841 rocket booster, using the space for more fuel and two DEFA 552 30 mm cannon, with 125 rounds per gun. The original Mirage's external payload options included just a single MATRA R.530 air-to-air missile (AAM) under the fuselage, plus two wing hardpoints limited to carrying external fuel tanks for ferrying purposes. Yet Israeli Mirage IIIs were able to carry two 500-kg bombs under the fuselage, while the wet-wing stations were modified for a single 500-kg weapon each. Two outer wing stations were added for infrared AAMs.

TROUBLESOME INTRODUCTION

The first IDF/AF unit to operate the Shahak (Skyblazer), as the Mirage III became known in Israel, was No 101 Sqn. The first two examples were flown from France to Hatzor on 7 April 1962. Deliveries to the second IDF/AF fighter unit commenced on 7 July when four arrived at Ramat David to join No 117 Sqn. Both units were intended to become masters of all trades, the Shahak performing both air-to-air and air-to-ground mission, as well as replacing Meteor and Vautour nightfighters. New weapons and tactics were to be devised and implemented, although the Shahak initially suffered from immature technology.

In some ways the Mirage III was a masterpiece, being perhaps the most sleek and aerodynamically-designed of all first-generation Mach 2 fighters. Its powerplant and the weapons system, however, were considerably inferior to equivalent US and UK products. Indeed, no fewer than four Shahaks were lost during 1963 in accidents related to engine malfunctions, the problem soon being traced to the Atar 9B-3's accessory box. Although none was lost due to weapon system faults, the unreliability of the latter nevertheless caused much frustration among Israeli pilots.

Advertised as a revolutionary fighting machine capable of being operated by a single pilot in all weather conditions, the initial disappointment caused by the Shahak was tremendous. At first it became obvious that Mach 2 performance was irrelevant in traditional dogfights, and this was especially true in combat with 'inferior' fighters.

Although the comparable MiG-21 began to enter Egyptian service in May 1962, few of the Shahak's opponents in the Middle East fell into this Mach 2 category. They were mostly MiG-17s and MiG-19s, but also Hunters and, from

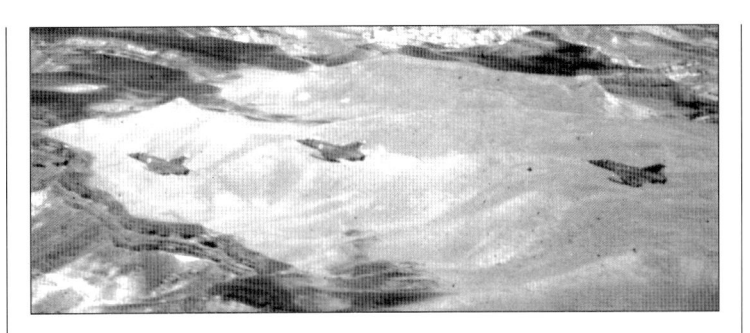

Adopting low-level flight profiles was the only practical way of avoiding early detection by hostile radar systems that ringed the Israeli border

The Cyrano radar represented a landmark in IDF/AF history because it introduced a multi-mode system as standard equipment in its combat aircraft. Following the service entry of the F-4 in 1969, the Cyrano was then employed purely in the range-finding role, although it was later removed from all Shahaks and replaced by ballast. Throughout its 20 years of service, the Mirage III underwent just four major technical changes in IDF/AF service – the introduction of the 'holding switches', replacement of the Cyrano with ballast, swapping the Atar 9B for the 9C and, finally, removal of part of the ballast at ace Kobi Richter's request in 1977. This moved the centre of gravity backwards, cutting minimum speed from 150 to 120 knots and increasing maximum 'G' from 6.5 to 7.3, thus improving sustained turn rates

A hit but not a kill. No 101 Sqn's Amos Amir engaged a Syrian MiG-21 on 14 November 1964, but suffered failure with all three weapons types at his disposal. The Cyrano did not lock so the R.530 could not be used, the Shafrir homed on to the ground and the cannon shells hit the MiG-21 but did not inflict fatal damage

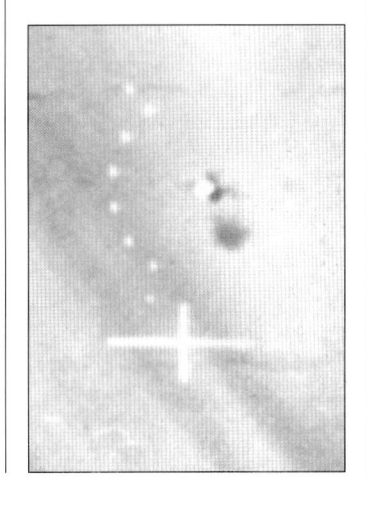

1967 onwards, Su-7s as well. The Hunter and the MiG-17 had astonishing air combat performance, and when Shahak pilots practiced their superior-inferior combat against IDF/AF Super Mysteres, it became apparent that new tactics were required to ensure that the deltas' supposed superiority would indeed result in defeating the inferior fighter, and not vice versa.

As these adversaries, other than the MiG-19 and Su-7, had superior subsonic turn performance, the emerging Shahak air combat tactics focused on maximising the Mach 2 fighter's strengths – sheer speed, acceleration and rate of climb. The preferred tactic was a sort of 'hit and run', which meant using initial ground control vectoring to achieve surprise, preferably from as far away as possible, through the launching of an air-to-air missile (AAM). Shahak pilots would close to cannon range only if the AAM missed, which often happened in those days.

If forced to dogfight an inferior opponent, the best tactic was to preserve a higher energy state by climbing or diving, rather than by turning with the enemy, thereby bleeding energy and losing the advantage of speed. To Israeli pilots, the use of the vertical dimension became known as 'stitching', for in such conditions a fighter's trajectory in combat often resembled the movement of a hand stitching with needle and thread.

Such tactics took time to evolve and perfect, and were greatly hampered by the effectiveness of the Shahak's weapon system. Tracing its origins to point defence against bombers equipped with nuclear weapons, the

Shahak's weapon system was supposed to incorporate cutting-edge technology. This would have been true if the equipment had worked as advertised, but it rarely did. The CSF Cyrano radar was designed to lock onto a relatively large target flying at high altitude during an interception in which the radar was 'looking' upwards. Once lock-on was achieved, the radar-slaved CSF-95 gunsight acquired the target and the cannon were automatically triggered at a range of 700 m. Theoretically, it was a fantastic system, but in reality nothing worked.

In a look-down situation, with the Shahak above the target, the Cyrano was unable to acquire anything below 30,000 ft over land – or 10,000 ft over the sea – due to ground clutter. Unacceptable low serviceability due to overheating did not encourage confidence in the new system either. In fact, throughout the Shahak's service career, only a few aerial kills resulted from a proper lock-on which delivered accurate range data to the gunsight. The Cyrano was retained because it was already installed and nothing else was available, but it was only considered useful in maritime night attacks which conferred upon Shahak units a unique operational competence, and provided the IDF/AF with limited capability in this area.

A mid-1960s project to improve Cyrano performance was contracted to IAI Elta, but was scrapped by the end of the decade following delivery of US combat aircraft with superior radar systems. The Cyrano radars were removed shortly afterwards and replaced by a ballast weight.

Manual Cannon Aiming

Different types of aircraft suffer differing levels of vulnerability to battle damage. The MiG-17, the Hunter and the Su-7 could take plenty of punishment, but a single well-placed hit could easily turn a MiG-21 into a spectacular fireball. Air combat tactics in the 1960s dictated three principle phases to achieve a kill, although only the last was absolutely essential to success. These phases were clever ground control vectoring towards the enemy aircraft to place the fighter in an advantageous position, superior tactics to gain a firing position and the infliction of lethal damage.

IDF/AF ground control tactics were honed to perfection and the Shahak pilots' air combat tactics were of the highest possible standard, but hitting the target remained the key issue. Initially, Shahak hit rates during

These No 101 Sqn Shahaks are seen lined up as part of the unit's 15th anniversary celebrations on 29 May 1963

Efraim Ashkenazi (back row extreme left) was an Ouragan OTU instructor during 1961/62 (Term 3) when the graduates of fighter school class 35 attended his unit. The five instructors for the course are standing at the back of this group shot, and they are, from left to right Ashkenazi, Shabtai Gilboa, Arlozor Lev (squadron CO), Ran Alon and Amos Amir. The 12 students are (seated, middle row, from left to right) Moshe Heichal, Mordechai Pinto, Avraham Salmon, Avner Slapak, Rafi Lev and Boaz Gafni, and kneeling (from left to right) Amram Zecharya, Eliezer Magid, Gidon Dror, Oded Zakai, Yitzhak Barzilai and Yair Neuman. Half of the graduates were killed in flying accidents and combat, Neuman and Pinto dying in the Six Day War, Lev being killed in the Yom Kippur War and Gafni, Zakai and Zecharya perishing in flying accidents. Six of these 17 pilots were to be credited with kills, and three – Salmon, Amir and Dror – became aces practice air-to-air gunnery drills were embarrassingly low – an average of only 1.9 per cent was recorded in the first term of training. Inevitably, this result was attributed to the inexperience of pilots on a new type, to the higher closing rates resulting from the Shahak's superior performance, and to the deficiencies of the weapon system that made lock-on almost impossible, especially in a dogfight.

Although the build-up of experience on the Shahak, and intensive air-to-air gunnery training, resulted in constant improvement (up to an average of 22 per cent), there were basic flaws in the system. The Shahaks' inability to shoot down enemy aircraft in at least four air combats between August 1963 and March 1965 certainly highlighted the problem. Pilots did not hit the enemy aircraft, and when they did, lethal damage was not inflicted. The later problem was easily solved when it was realised that as a bomber interceptor, the rounds fired by the Mirage were optimised to explode inside a large target. Upon hitting a small tactical fighter the round penetrated, exited and exploded beyond, inflicting only light damage, rather than ensuring a kill. The obvious cure was to use zero delay-fused rounds that exploded on impact.

Improving aiming required a rather more ingenious solution. This was provided by an IDF/AF group called the 'Shahak Zeroing Team', led by IDF/AF Air 2 (Weapon Systems Branch, Air Department's second branch) staff officer Efraim Ashkenazi, who was an electronics engineer and No 101 Sqn Shahak pilot. The inaccuracy of the fighter's weapon system was so profound that the difference between the true aiming point and that of the gunsight was six milirads. This was a significant deviation given that the diameter of the aiming point was only two milirads.

French manufacturer CSF was developing a modification, but it was the 'Shahak Zeroing Team' which saved the day. Its interim solution was simple, and although the 'fix' represented a step backwards, it worked. In fact the solution worked so well that it was never replaced. Two switches were installed on the control column. One provided a 250 m range gunsight firing solution, while the other fixed the sight at 400 m, with the activation of both set at 600 m. In the heat of air combat, pilots had only to roughly estimate the range to the target – close, medium or long – activate the appropriate switch and open fire.

Scramble! No 101 Sqn pilot Avshalom Ran dashes to Shahak 52, which is armed with an R.530 Yahalom AAM on the centreline pylon. The jet also carries a ubiquitous 500-litre supersonic fuel tank under each wing

In the days before instrumented air combat manoeuvring training, a pilot was credited with a 'kill' in a training sortie if he preserved a perfect firing solution for one second. Gunsight cameras filmed at 16 frames per second, so a pilot had to present at least 16 consecutive frames. As most of the sortie was not captured on film, training sessions were analysed, lessons were learned and skills were honed during the 'balcony debrief'. Pictured here in 1963 are No 101 Sqn pilots Ran Ronen, Oded Marom, Dan Sever and Moti Yeshurun

The Shahak's cockpit was dominated by the gunsight at the pilot's eye level and by the radar scope, positioned immediately behind the control column. The fuel gauge was to the right of the radar scope and the external stores selectors to the left. The Mirage III was a pilot's machine, as Gidon Dror recalled. 'When we strapped in we felt as if we were "wearing" the aircraft. It was as though you had become one with the jet'

The Shahak represented a quantum leap in both technology and performance for the IDF/AF, and training pilots to fly it was not a straightforward procedure. To make matters worse no two-seaters were available until 1966, so pilots learned about the jet's very sensitive control system, which could easily be mishandled, inducing an uncontrollable oscillation, on their own. The fighter could also be 'skittish' on landing, as Shahak 22 of No 117 Sqn proved when it veered off the runway. On this occasion the damage was minimal. Reassigned to No 119 Sqn after being repaired, it was involved in the first fatal Shahak accident when Ya'acov Berman was killed during air base attack practice on 24 August 1966

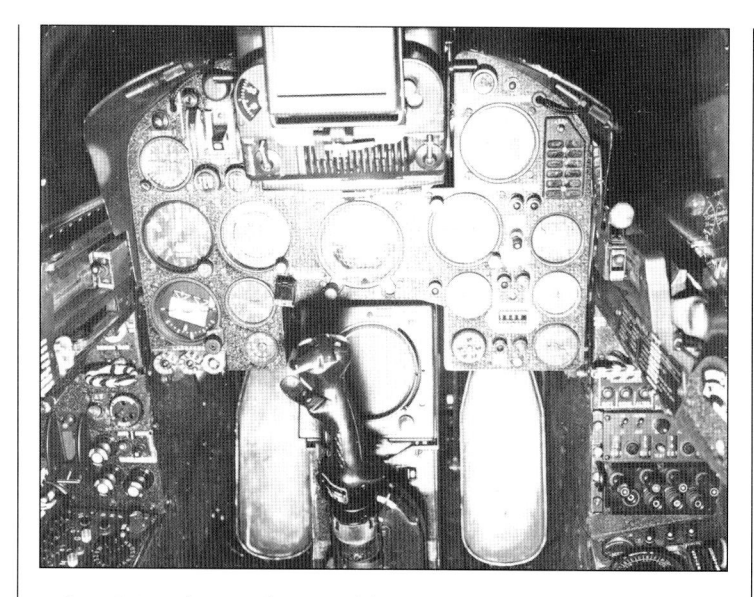

In training, the introduction of the 'holding switches', as Shahak pilots called the modification, immediately raised the air-to-air hit rate to 35 per cent. Far more significant was the fact that in less than a year the Shahaks were to be credited with 11 kills. Efraim Ashkenazi won the 1968 Israel Defence Award, the highest honour presented by the State of Israel in recognition of technological achievements contributing to national security. Ashkenazi died of cancer on 15 December 1969, aged just 31. However, by the time of his death the Shahaks had already downed 100 enemy aircraft, and most of these kills were due to his 'holding switches'. It is hard to estimate the extent to which Ashkenazi's exposure to the components of the Cyrano radar during his work contributed to his fatal illness.

THE OPENING ELEVEN

Yoram Agmon graduated as part of IDF/AF Flying School (FS) Class 36 in March 1962. By July 1966 he was an instructor, and also flying the Shahak with No 101 Sqn as an emergency posting (EP) pilot. IDF/AF units included four principle categories of aircrew – the management (CO and two deputies), regular, EP and reserve. In the early 1960s all IDF/AF aircrews were required to become FS instructors as part of their career development. They continued to fly with their old frontline units as EPs, joining the squadron for one day a week in order to maintain competence. During exercises, periods of tension and war, EPs were the first to reinforce frontline units, as reservists were called up only when absolutely essential.

On 13 July 1966, an IDF vehicle was destroyed by a mine close to the Syrian border. Three Israelis were killed and retaliation was inevitable.

The following morning high alert status was announced, and EP aircrews were called to their squadrons. At 1600 hrs IDF/AF jets attacked Syrian targets, with two Shahak four-ship formations flying combat air patrol (CAP) for the attack aircraft. Dan Sever, No 101 Sqn's senior deputy commander, led Avner Slapak, Oded Sagi and Yoram Agmon (in Shahak 59) in one of the CAP formations. Agmon recalled;

'We returned from lunch and there was a four-ship formation planned for a CAP, but the pilot scheduled to fly as No 4 had to go somewhere so I became No 4. We replaced another CAP and were patrolling along the Golan Heights on our side of the border when the controller ordered "full power west". I knew the aircraft quite well, and I knew that with large external fuel tanks, flying with or without afterburner was roughly the same. Maybe I would lag behind a little, but as No 4 I was entitled to, so I was the only one who did not fly with afterburner. Then the controller ordered us to turn east and I had 300-400 litres of fuel more than the others. As we headed east I saw two MiGs at low altitude. We were flying at 20,000 ft. I reported, lowered my nose and jettisoned the external tanks. I felt I must not lose them because they were tiny dots. But I did lose them. I decided to dive to the lowest altitude I could and acquire them in the same direction above the horizon. That's exactly what happened.

'As I levelled out I saw them about two kilometres ahead. When I was behind them – not yet in range to open fire – and at that altitude, there was no AAM option. They broke hard. Maybe someone warned them. Their break surprised me. It was a beautiful turn, a great break, but it gave me the opportunity to close the distance. I was in a position on the leading MiG. The trailing MiG was in the area, but not in the picture, and probably never saw me. I opened fire but missed. My second or third burst hit the wing. It immediately spun in and exploded. The pilot ejected. I saw the empty cockpit and watched it crash. It happened at an altitude of about 500 ft. The other pilots landed at Ramat David due to fuel shortages, but I was able to fly to Hatzor, where there was great joy.   I don't know if it's true, but the groundcrew counted the cannon rounds and said I had expended exactly 101.'

The first victory came as a relief to an IDF/AF leadership, which had put its trust in the French delta-fighter. Moreover, the kill was achieved with cannon – a supposedly obsolete weapon only installed in an advanced fighting machine at IDF/AF insistence. Above all, Agmon's achievement was the first in a series of victories which was to create the Mirage legend, and turn a troublesome fighter into a weapon of deterrence. The MiG-21 and the Mirage III were comparable, although the Soviet design had a distinct advantage in several key areas, yet the Shahak's superiority could not have gone unnoticed by Arab pilots. Now every one entering combat with a Shahak would be aware of the Israeli fighter's superiority. So profound was its impact that the Mirage would become a 'must have' fighter for a number of Arab air forces.

The Shahak's amazing air-to-air results can be attributed to rigorous training and coherent tactics that were honed to perfection. Serving with only three squadrons (No 119 Sqn was formed in 1964 at Tel Nof as the third Shahak unit), there were never more than 100 active Shahak pilots at any one time. They were, though, specialists in air-to-air combat. They flew other missions, but the reason they were selected to fly the aircraft was

No 101 Sqn organised the 1965/66 Term 2 conversion course, and the pilots involved are seen here in front of the unit's distinctive emblem. They are, from left to right (standing), Ilan Gonen, David Baruch, Avraham Oren and Yossi Arazi, and sitting (from left to right) Ehud Henkin, Giora Rom, Moshe Gilboa, Ilan Hait and David Porat. Five of these pilots were to be credited with kills, and two, Gonen and Rom, became aces. Baruch was killed in the Six Day War, Henkin died in the Yom Kippur War and Gilboa was lost in a flying accident

The Shahak's first combat kill. The gunsight film from 14 July 1966 reveal's Yoram Agmon's aiming-point to be the right wing. There is a noticeable shuddering in this frame, caused by the firing of Shahak 59's 30 mm cannon. The rounds hit the Syrian MiG-21 in the left wing root, causing the jet to erupt in flames

CHAPTER ONE

No 117 Sqn conducted the 1966/67 Term 3 conversion course. The eight pilots pictured in the centre are (from left to right) Eli Zohar, Shlomo Egozi, Amichai Roke'ach, Omri Afek, Amos Cohen, Yuval Ne'eman, Ron Holdai and Arnon Levoshin. Standing (from left to right) are Amichai Shamueli (CO), Shlomo Navot, Amit Livni, Avi Lanir, Yehuda Koren, Uri Liss, Amnon Gardi, Uri Dekel (navigator), Meir Livneh, Reuven Har'el, Avraham Oren, Ezra Dotan, Uri Aven-Nir, Yigal Yanai, Adi Benaya, Naftali Porat, Shraga Pessach and Dror Avneri. Meir Shachar, Shlomo Nir and Gidon Dror are in the bottom row

Each unit had several hardened aircraft shelters, plus an alert complex with five armed Shahaks – two pairs and a spare – under sun-shelters. These aircraft belong to No 119 Sqn

their proficiency in this type of aerial fighting. This was to become even more pronounced after 1968, when the Shahak became a pure air-to-air fighter. The pilots' skills were combined with an extensive and advanced chain of ground control stations. The whole system was under constant training to perfect every conceivable aspect of air-to-air warfare.

Being numbered among the best heightened the desire to join what was considered to be an elite force. Yet during training, all pilots were seen as equal. The most senior pilots 'fought' the most junior during training in air combat manoeuvring. This attitude resulted in yet another force multiplier. Instead of the usual tactic of the wingman playing a solely defensive role, guarding his leader's tail during a dogfight, all Shahak pilots were trained to attack the enemy while still looking after each other.

Another skirmish along the Syrian border on 15 August 1966 resulted in the second Shahak kill when Yehuda Koren downed a Syrian MiG-21. The very next day brought the amazing sight of a Shahak escorting a MiG-21 into Hatzor. This was the result of a clandestine Mossad operation to deliver a MiG-21 to the IDF/AF by persuading an Iraqi pilot to defect with his aircraft. In the following months the Iraqi MiG-21 was extensively flight-tested to compare its performance with the Shahak. Ezra Aharon was one of the first six IDF/AF Shahak pilots, and as Air2 Head of Test Flight Section, he

IDF/AF chief test pilot Danny Shapira tested this Iraqi MiG-21 soon after it had defected in mid August 1966. There was a special emphasis made on comparing its performance with the Shahak

14

flew 13 comparison test flights between September and November 1966. He remembers;

'The Shahak had an angle of attack indicator (AoA) with changing lights – green, orange and red. As the AoA increased, the lights turned red, and officially it was not allowed to reach the pure red zone as there was a danger that the engine could stall and flame out. The MiG-21 had no such restriction. It could pitch its nose up sharply and, beyond a certain limit, the Shahak had to give up. In tight turns the MiG-21 was superior. In manoeuvrability the Shahak had the upper hand, being more agile.'

The knowledge gathered was spread among the Shahak pilots. The MiG-21's major weak spots were summarised as poor pilot visibility, limited endurance and the hazard caused by the proximity of the oxygen tank to the engine starter's high-octane fuel tank. Although this information might not seem valuable in combat, it gave Shahak pilots an insight into what was going on in the cockpit of their main adversary. This gave the Israelis a psychological advantage, for not only were Shahak pilots shooting down MiG-21s, they were also intimately familiar with it. There was no trick that could surprise them and Arab MiG-21 pilots knew that.

The third Shahak kill was a Jordanian Hunter downed on 13 November 1966 by Ran Ronen in No 119 Sqn's Shahak 84. Thirteen days later, two important events in the jet's history occurred when No 101 Sqn pilot Michael 'Diamond' Haber downed two Egyptian MiG-19s. This was the first double Shahak kill, and the first by an R.530 Yahalom AAM.

The AAM was not yet a mature weapon, and it was not until the service introduction of more reliable missiles in 1969 that it would offer a viable alternative to the cannon. Two types were initially available to Shahak pilots – the semi-active radar homing (SARH) Yahalom and the infrared (IR) Rafael Shafrir (Dragonfly). Seven Shafrirs were launched in air combat between November 1964 and April 1967 and all missed. The Yahalom was rather more successful, with a 50 per cent success rate – two launched for a single kill.

The number of Shahak kills more than doubled on 7 April 1967 when a major skirmish along the Syrian border resulted in six victories. This was the day of the first shared kill by Shahak pilots when No 101 Sqn's Yiftach Spector and Beni Romach claimed a MiG-21 between them after Spector had downed one single-handedly. The other successful pilots were No 119 Sqn CO Ran Ronen, who was credited with his second kill, No 117 Sqn's Ezra Dotan and Avi Lanir, and No 101 Sqn's Avner Slapak, who later recalled;

'We were patrolling along the border when I saw a glittering object far away over the Golan Heights. I reported to the controller and he told me, "you may attack". I applied full afterburner, heading east. The MiGs entered the Valley of the Yarmouk River, so I climbed and for a moment lost sight of them. But I guessed their flight path and flew

Ezra Aharon flew the Shahak between 1962 and 1982

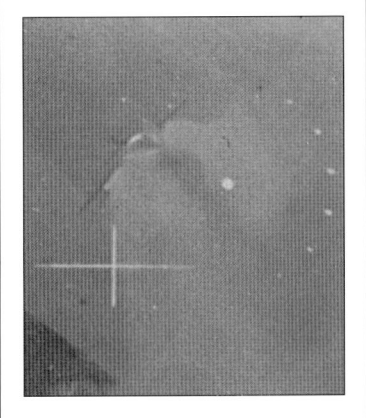

This gunsight camera frame from Shahak 84 reveals the last moments of the Jordanian Hunter downed by Ran Ronen on 13 November 1966

CO of No 119 Sqn, Ronen poses with his groundcrew beside Shahak 84 soon after claiming his Hunter kill – note the Jordanian flag beneath the cockpit

CHAPTER ONE

Avi Lanir's Shahak 60 was covered in soot after the Syrian MiG-21 that he was chasing blew up directly in front of him during the one-sided dogfight of 7 April 1967. Both of these aircraft (60 and 02) were duly lost in the Six Day War

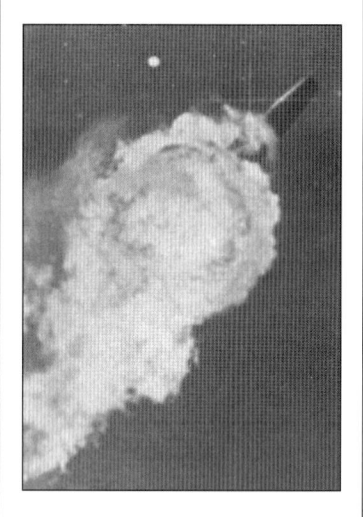

A MiG-21 bursts into flames after being hit by Ezra Dotan's cannon fire on 7 April 1967. A half-pressed trigger activated the gunsight camera. The aiming point is clearly visible above the MiG, revealing that Dotan has stopped firing and is now turning away so as to avoid hitting his victim

These No 101 Sqn Shahaks (09, 42, 51 and 52) are seen on 5 May 1967. The first two were lost three months later, while 51, credited with three kills and two shared, served the IDF/AF well until 1982

towards the canyon of the Yarmouk, where I saw them. They flew south-west and started to turn back to the right. I followed a MiG and he reversed. As I was starting to organise my gunsight, I heard shouts on the radio and noticed that there was shooting in the area.

'As I looked around, my first thought was that a MiG was chasing me. Then I saw a No 117 Sqn Shahak right above me, shooting. I switched to the common radio channel and said "Stop shooting. You are shooting at a friendly aircraft". I returned to my MiG (actually another one, because the MiG that Slapak had first chased was shot down by No 117 Sqn's Ezra Dotan), opened fire and observed hits. The pilot ejected and the MiG crashed on a hill east of El-Hama, on Jordanian soil.'

Claiming 11 kills within ten months was no mean feat. Ten fell to cannon fire, while a single AAM kill was also recorded. The victories were shared by all three Shahak units and ten pilots, thus widening the pool of combat experience. In addition to the shooting down of eight MiG-21s, the superior-inferior scenario was also tested in combat with victory over two MiG-19s and a single Hunter. With a single Shahak lost in November 1964 due to fuel starvation while returning from an engagement with a Jordanian Hunter, the Shahak kill-to-loss ratio stood at 11-to-1.

The loss of six MiG-21s on a single day was a severe blow to Arab honour and also to Soviet prestige. As a result, the Shahak's victory on 7 April 1967 triggered a diplomatic imbroglio that led to the Six Day War.

Colour Plates

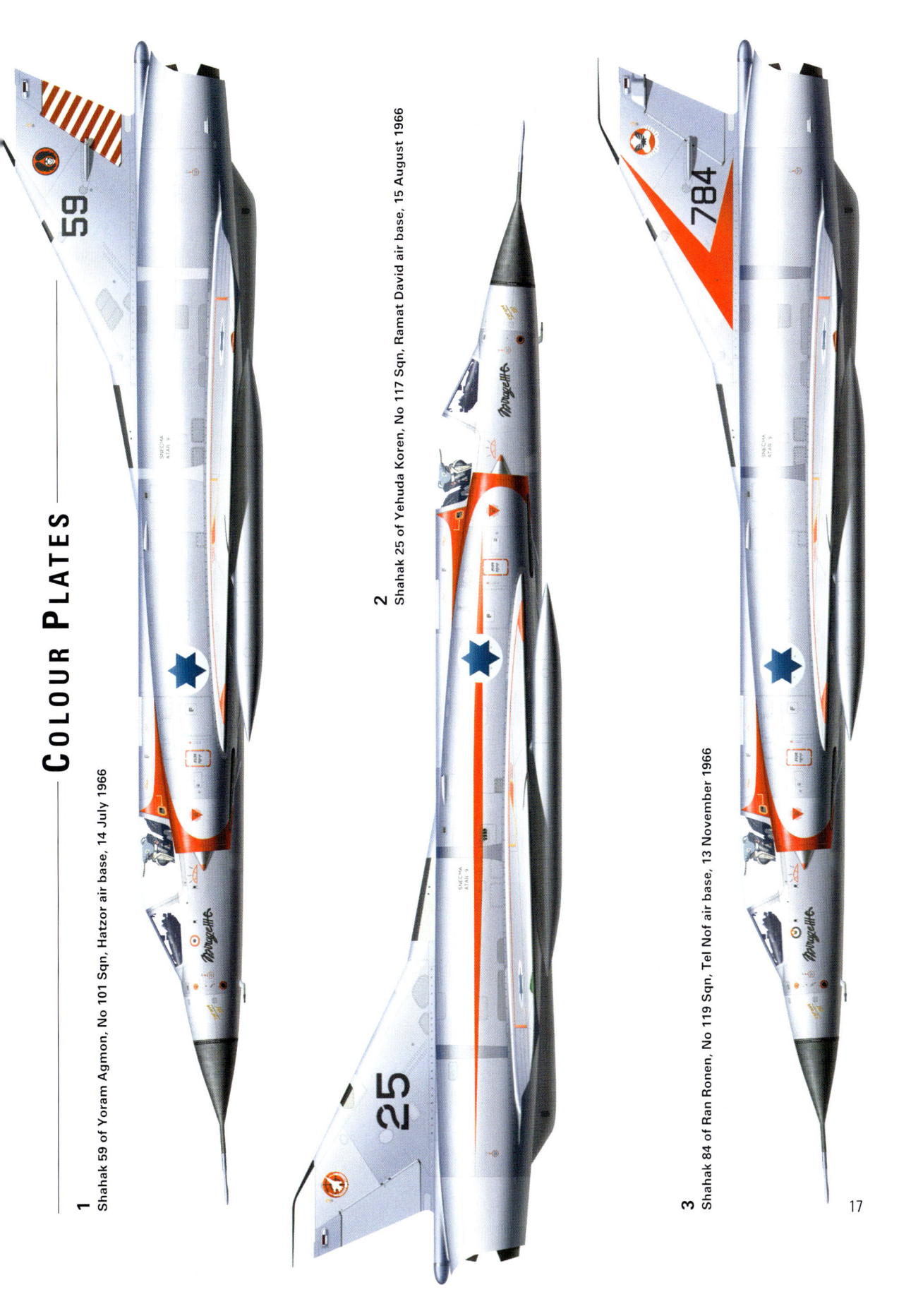

1
Shahak 59 of Yoram Agmon, No 101 Sqn, Hatzor air base, 14 July 1966

2
Shahak 25 of Yehuda Koren, No 117 Sqn, Ramat David air base, 15 August 1966

3
Shahak 84 of Ran Ronen, No 119 Sqn, Tel Nof air base, 13 November 1966

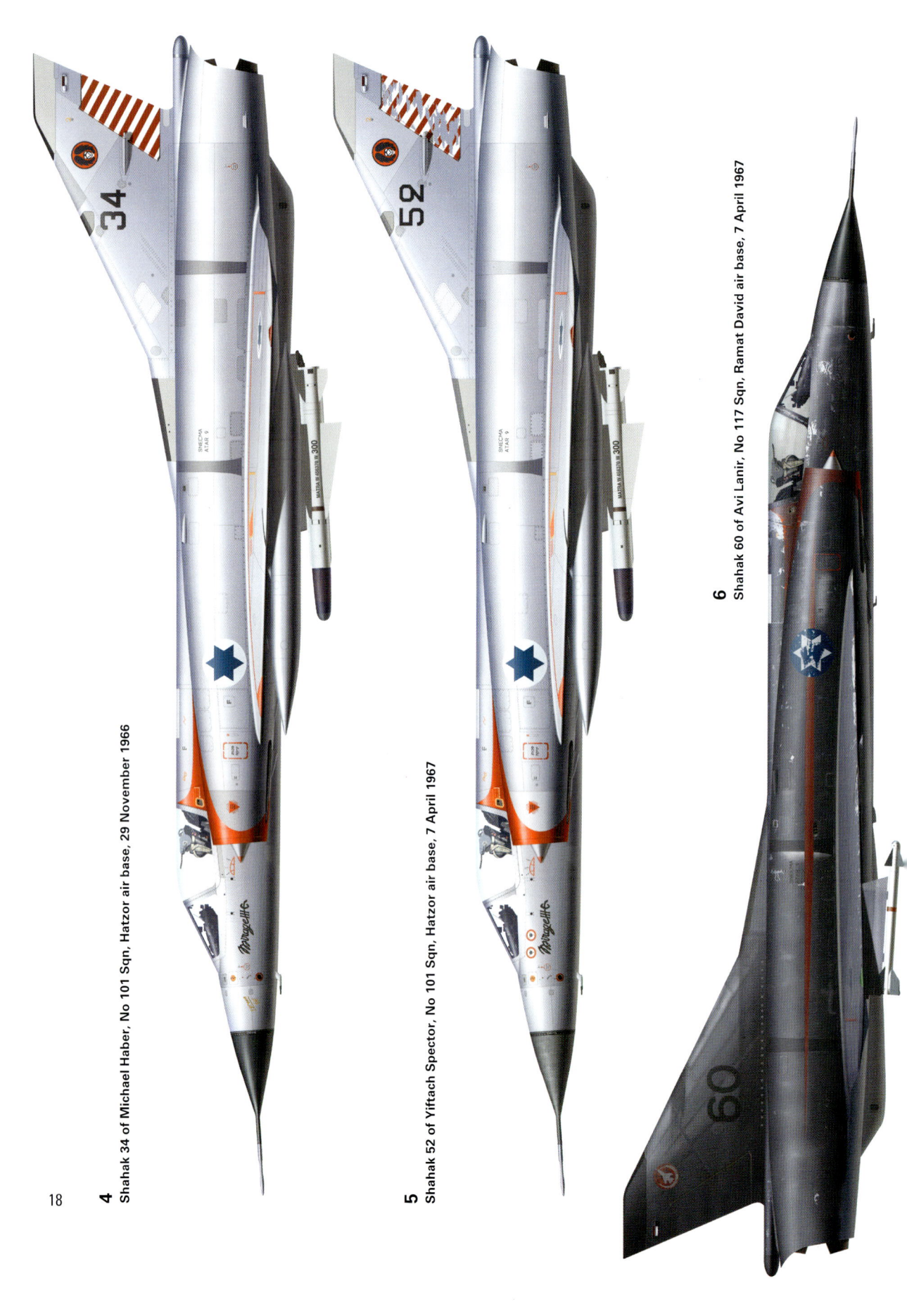

4
Shahak 34 of Michael Haber, No 101 Sqn, Hatzor air base, 29 November 1966

5
Shahak 52 of Yiftach Spector, No 101 Sqn, Hatzor air base, 7 April 1967

6
Shahak 60 of Avi Lanir, No 117 Sqn, Ramat David air base, 7 April 1967

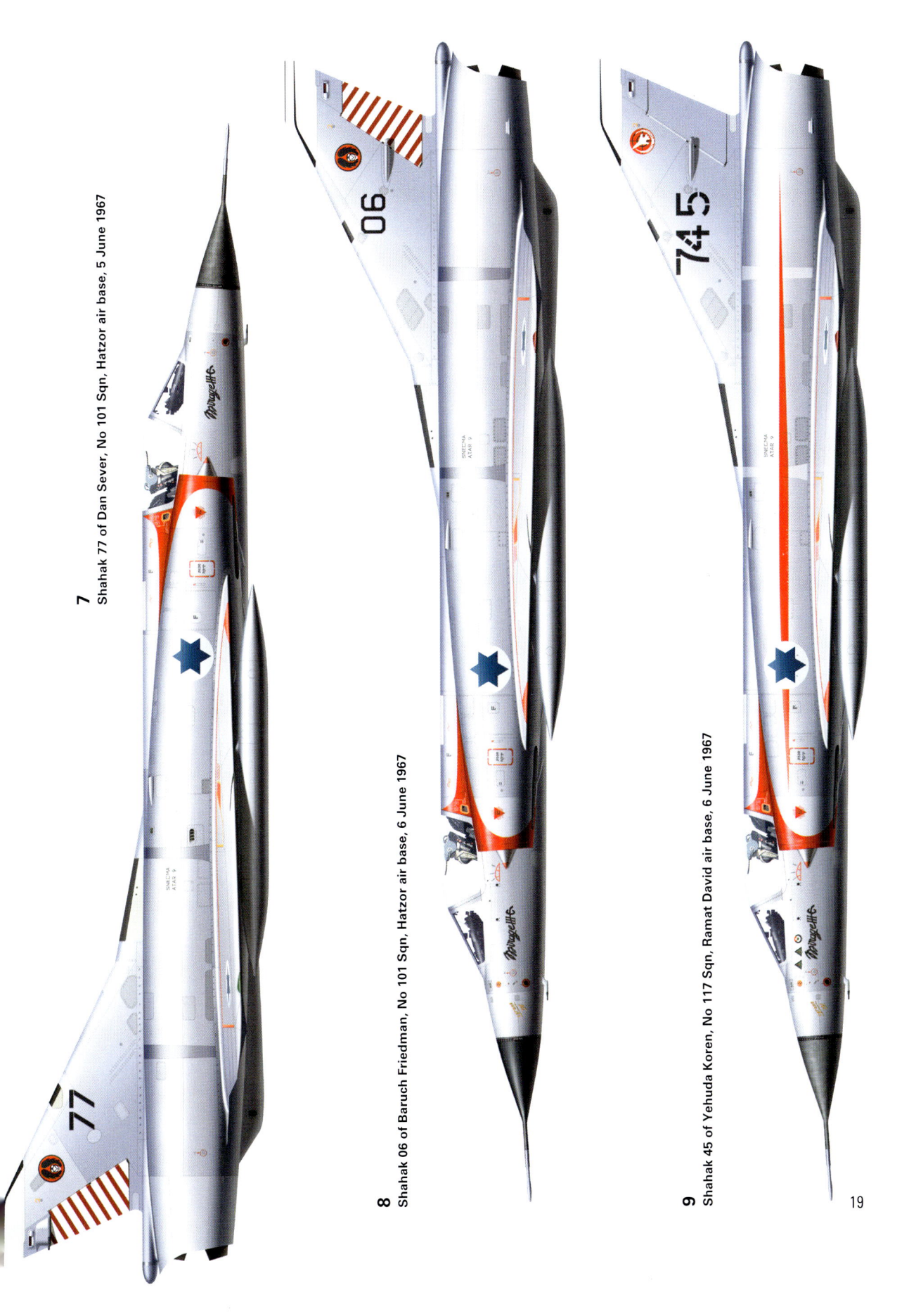

7
Shahak 77 of Dan Sever, No 101 Sqn, Hatzor air base, 5 June 1967

8
Shahak 06 of Baruch Friedman, No 101 Sqn, Hatzor air base, 6 June 1967

9
Shahak 45 of Yehuda Koren, No 117 Sqn, Ramat David air base, 6 June 1967

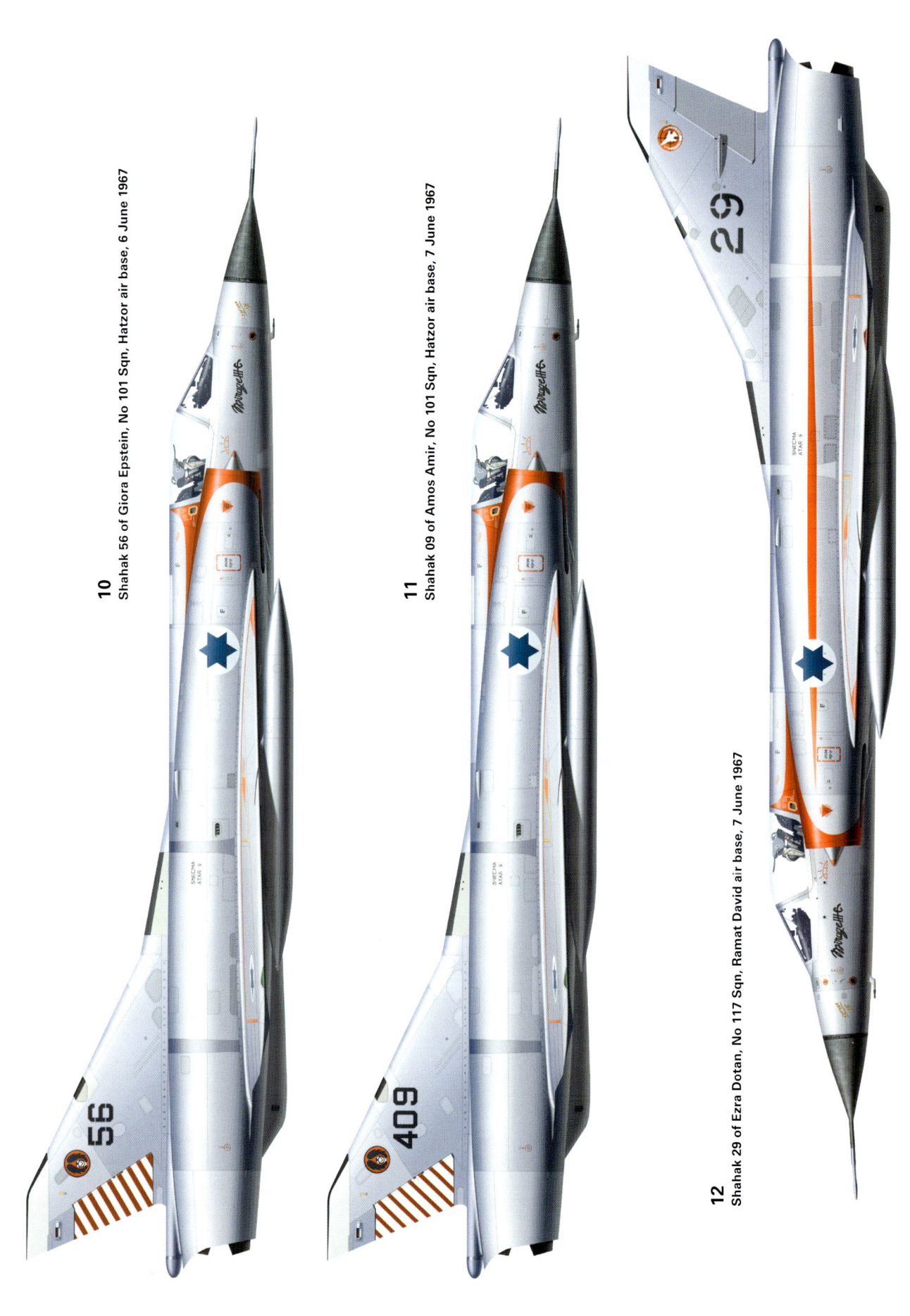

10
Shahak 56 of Giora Epstein, No 101 Sqn, Hatzor air base, 6 June 1967

11
Shahak 09 of Amos Amir, No 101 Sqn, Hatzor air base, 7 June 1967

12
Shahak 29 of Ezra Dotan, No 117 Sqn, Ramat David air base, 7 June 1967

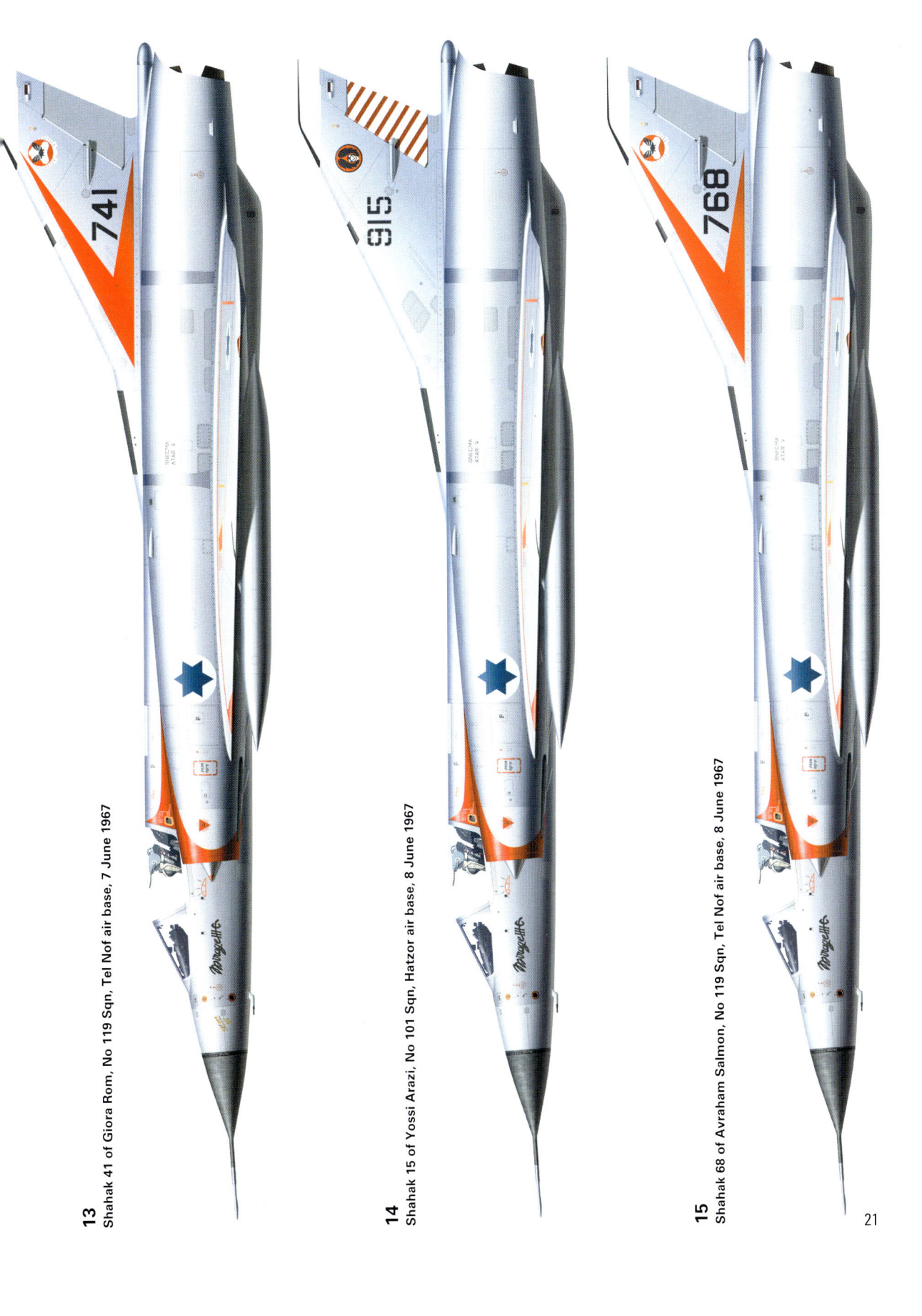

13
Shahak 41 of Giora Rom, No 119 Sqn, Tel Nof air base, 7 June 1967

14
Shahak 15 of Yossi Arazi, No 101 Sqn, Hatzor air base, 8 June 1967

15
Shahak 68 of Avraham Salmon, No 119 Sqn, Tel Nof air base, 8 June 1967

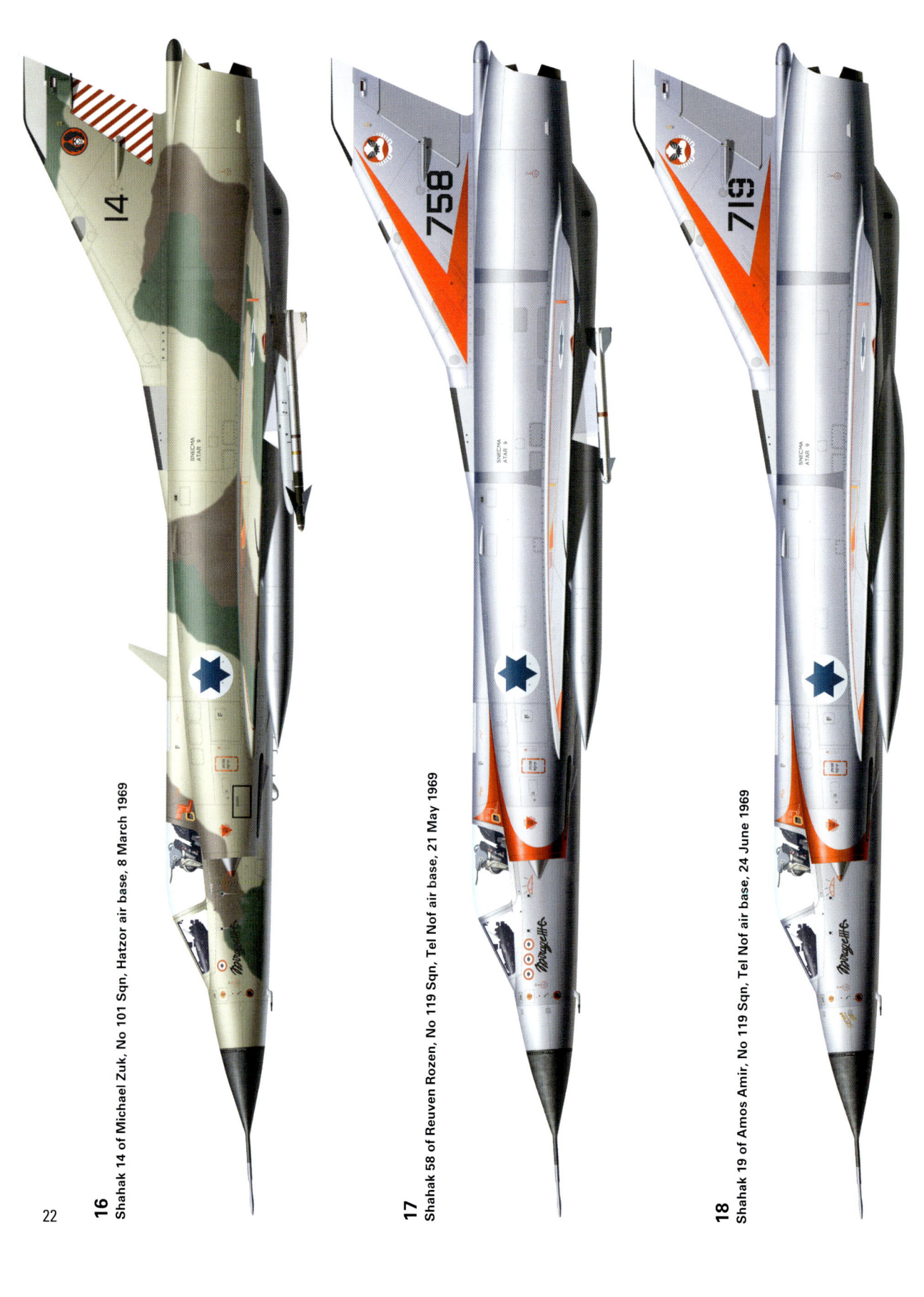

16
Shahak 14 of Michael Zuk, No 101 Sqn, Hatzor air base, 8 March 1969

17
Shahak 58 of Reuven Rozen, No 119 Sqn, Tel Nof air base, 21 May 1969

18
Shahak 19 of Amos Amir, No 119 Sqn, Tel Nof air base, 24 June 1969

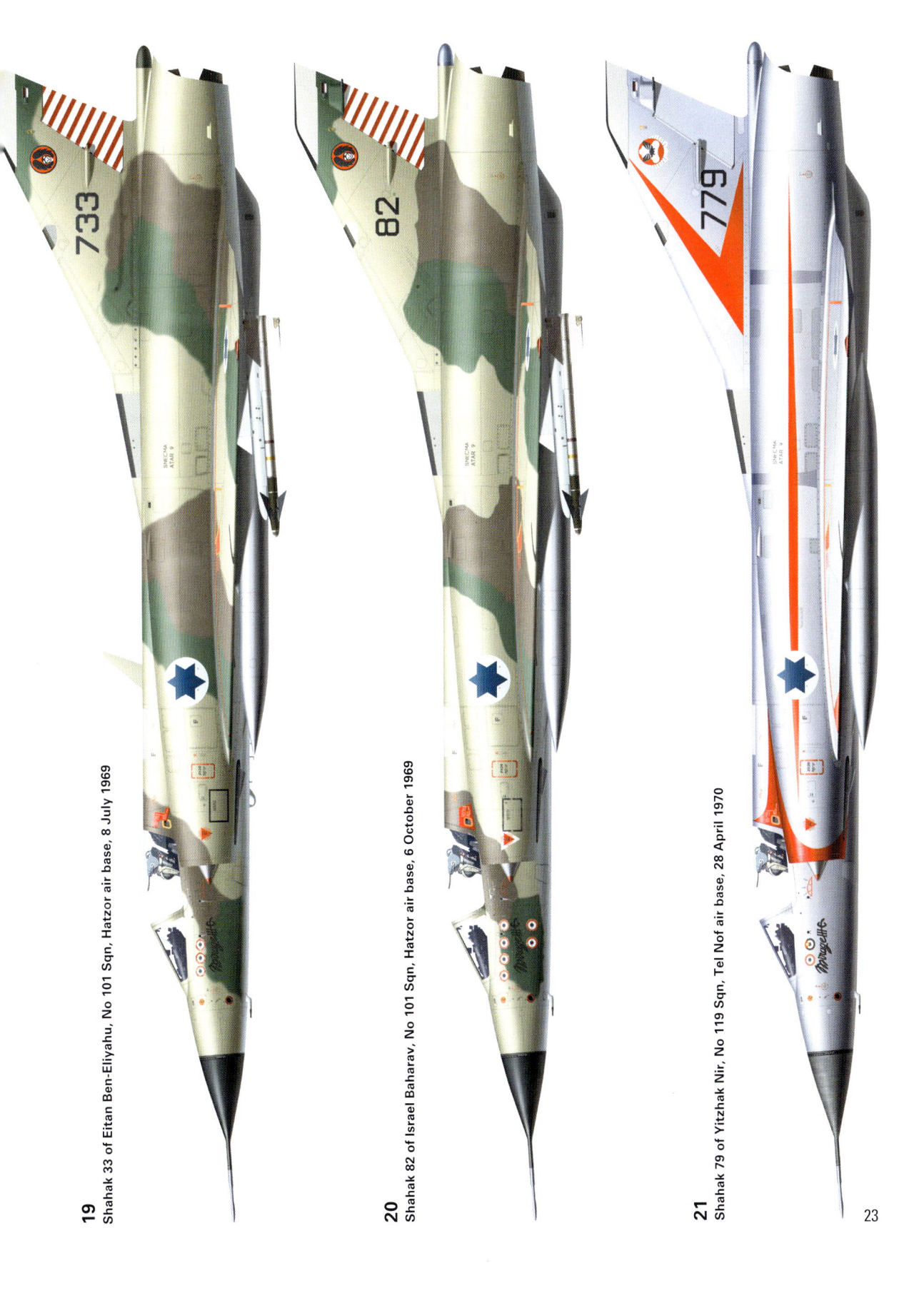

19
Shahak 33 of Eitan Ben-Eliyahu, No 101 Sqn, Hatzor air base, 8 July 1969

20
Shahak 82 of Israel Baharav, No 101 Sqn, Hatzor air base, 6 October 1969

21
Shahak 79 of Yitzhak Nir, No 119 Sqn, Tel Nof air base, 28 April 1970

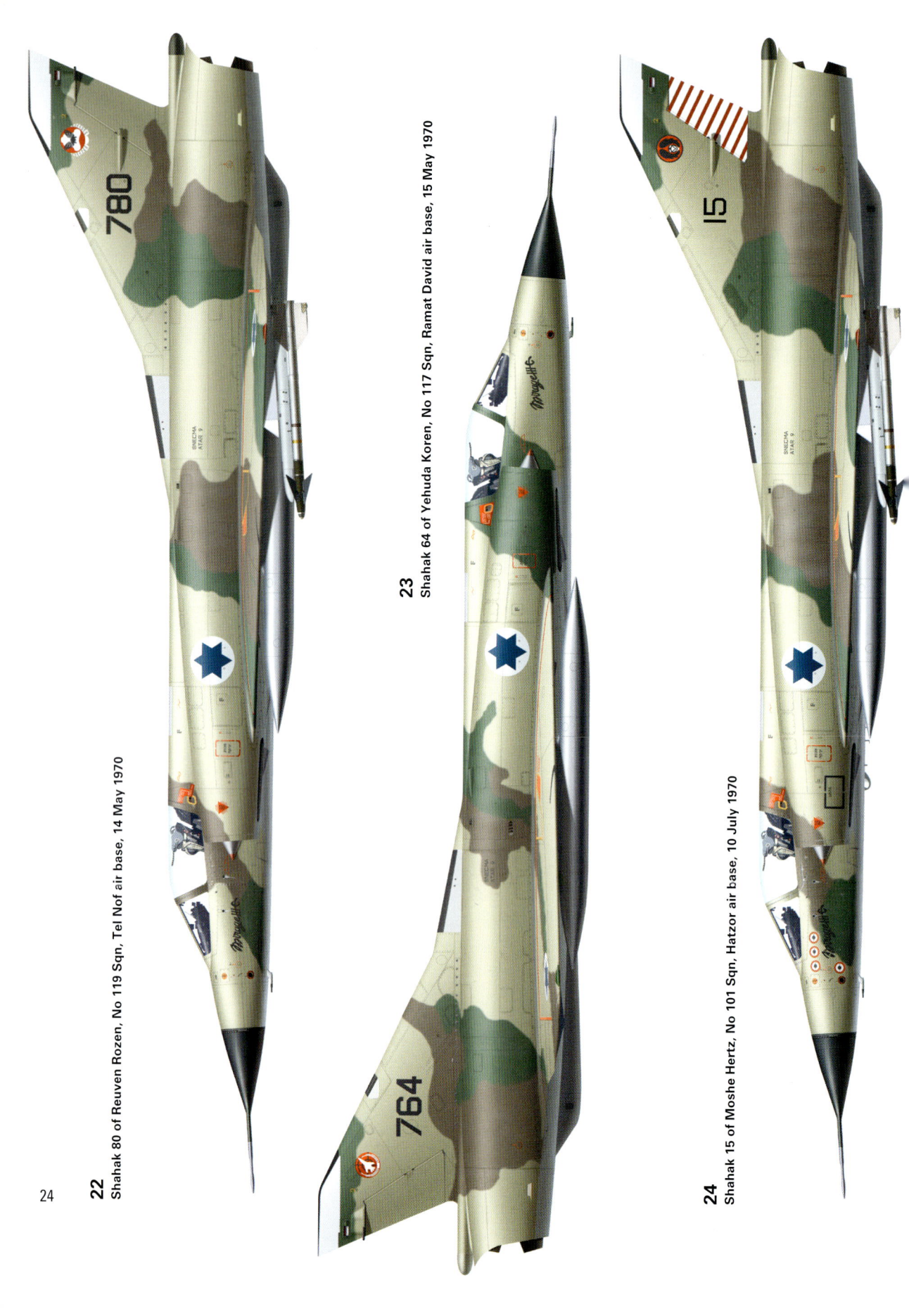

22
Shahak 80 of Reuven Rozen, No 119 Sqn, Tel Nof air base, 14 May 1970

23
Shahak 64 of Yehuda Koren, No 117 Sqn, Ramat David air base, 15 May 1970

24
Shahak 15 of Moshe Hertz, No 101 Sqn, Hatzor air base, 10 July 1970

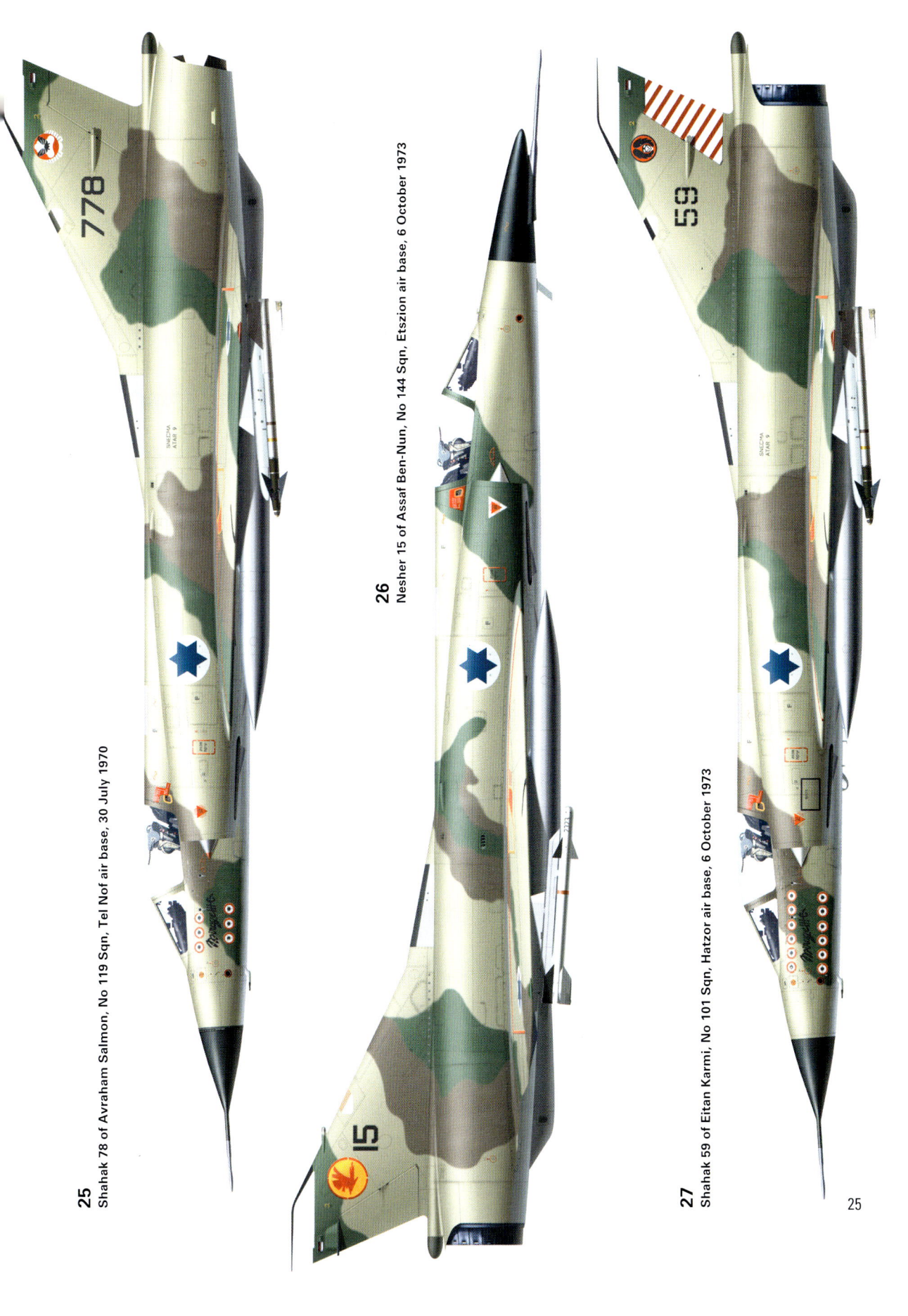

25
Shahak 78 of Avraham Salmon, No 119 Sqn, Tel Nof air base, 30 July 1970

26
Nesher 15 of Assaf Ben-Nun, No 144 Sqn, Etszion air base, 6 October 1973

27
Shahak 59 of Eitan Karmi, No 101 Sqn, Hatzor air base, 6 October 1973

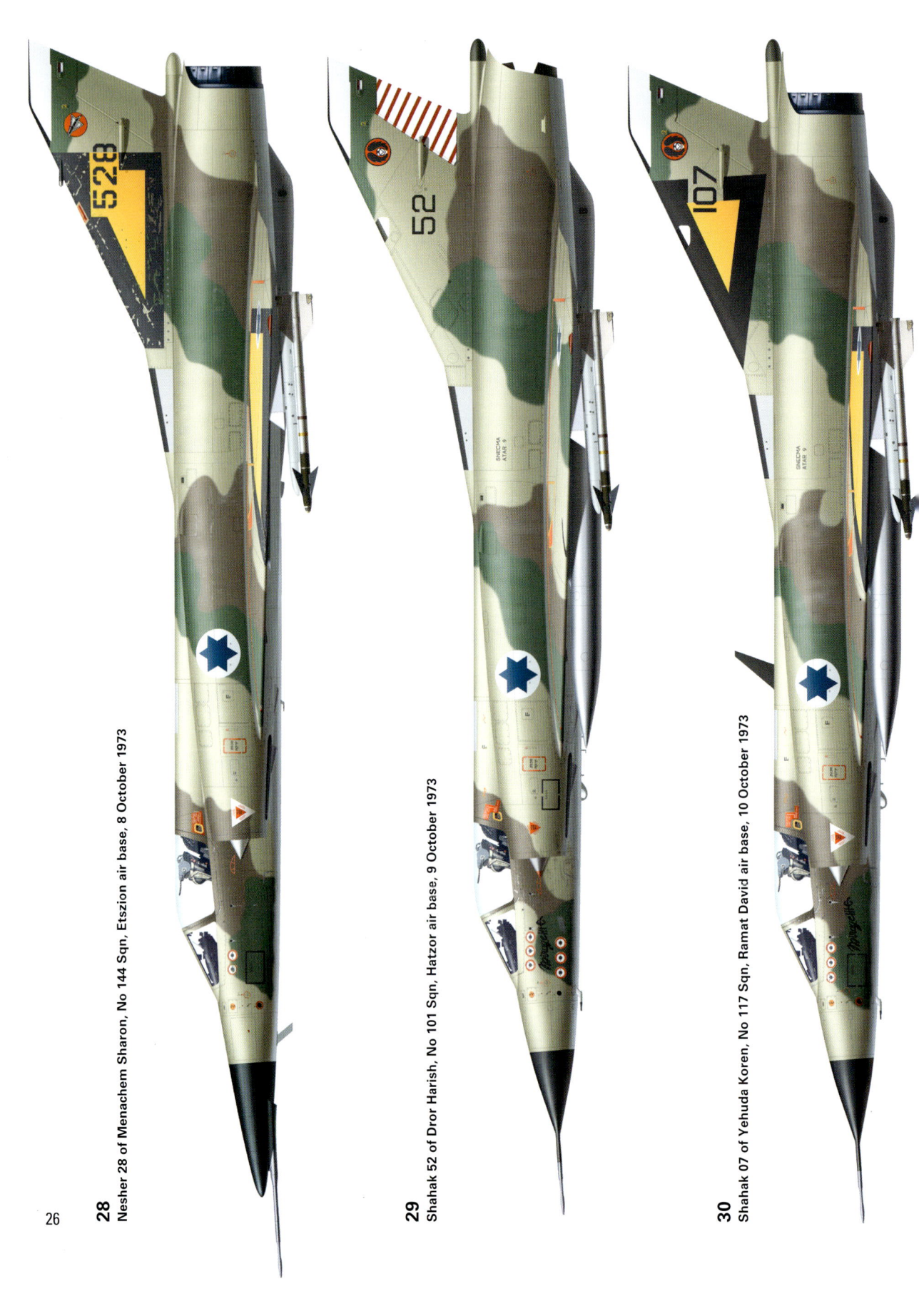

28
Nesher 28 of Menachem Sharon, No 144 Sqn, Etszion air base, 8 October 1973

29
Shahak 52 of Dror Harish, No 101 Sqn, Hatzor air base, 9 October 1973

30
Shahak 07 of Yehuda Koren, No 117 Sqn, Ramat David air base, 10 October 1973

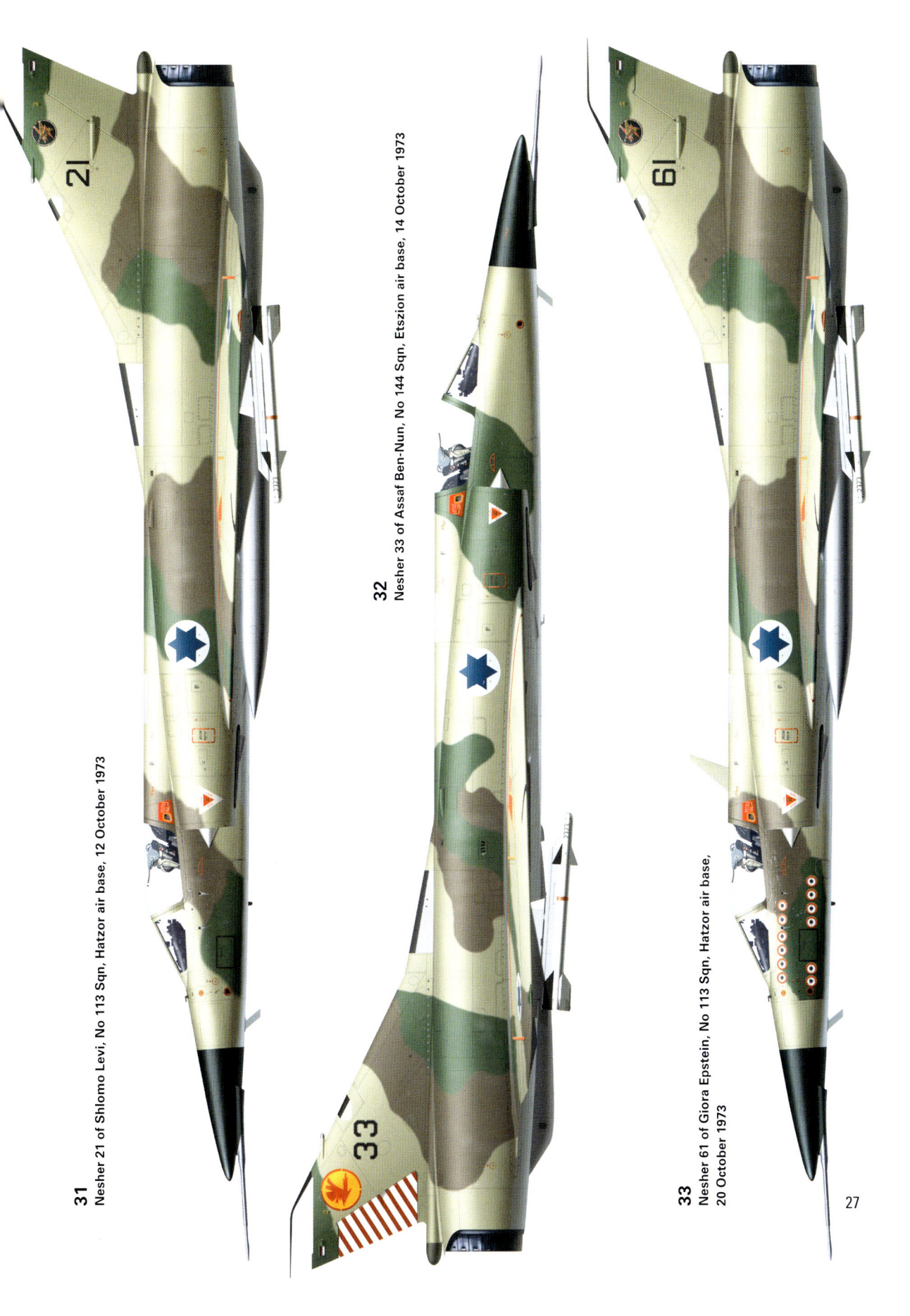

31
Nesher 21 of Shlomo Levi, No 113 Sqn, Hatzor air base, 12 October 1973

32
Nesher 33 of Assaf Ben-Nun, No 144 Sqn, Etszion air base, 14 October 1973

33
Nesher 61 of Giora Epstein, No 113 Sqn, Hatzor air base, 20 October 1973

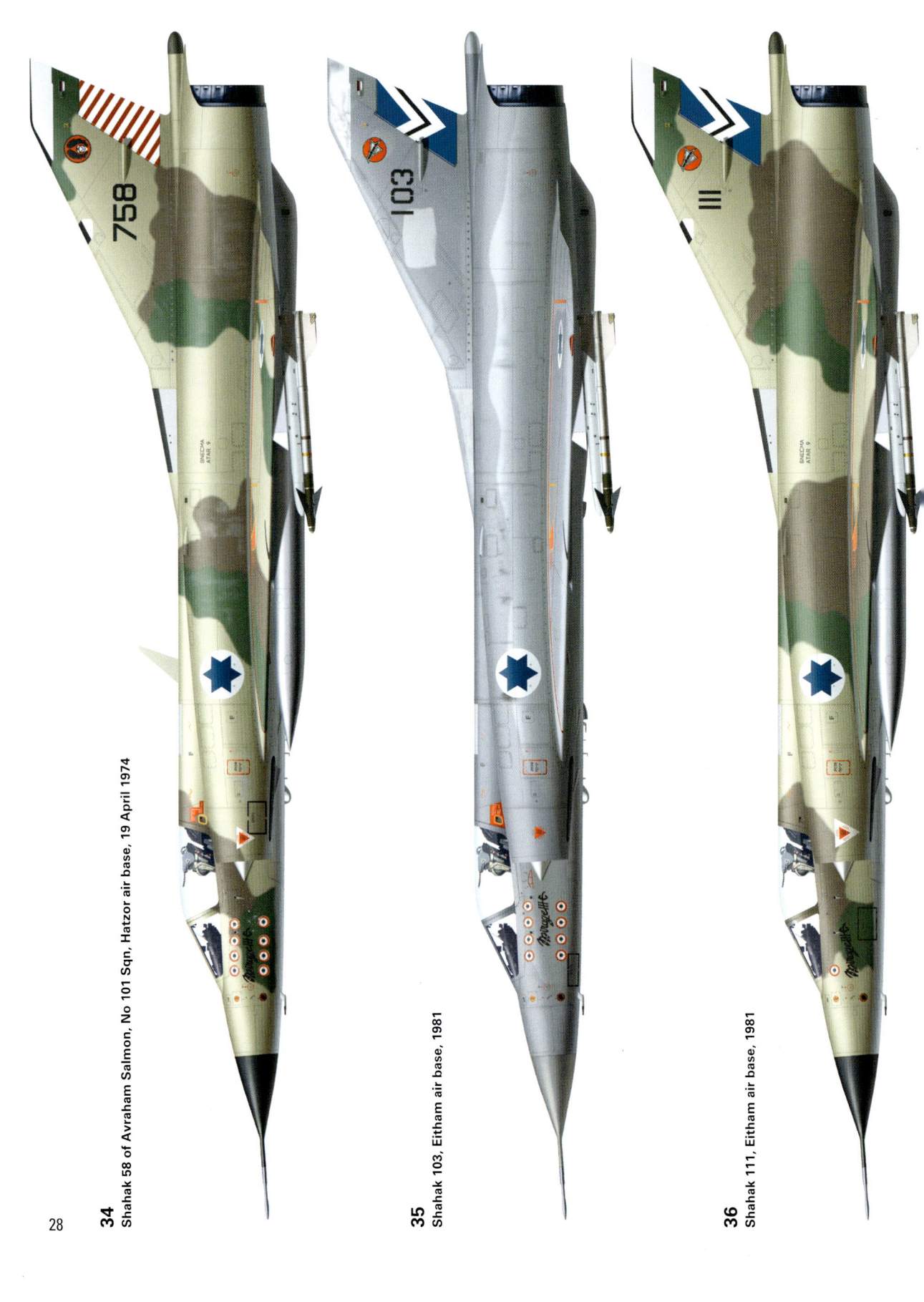

34
Shahak 58 of Avraham Salmon, No 101 Sqn, Hatzor air base, 19 April 1974

35
Shahak 103, Eitham air base, 1981

36
Shahak 111, Eitham air base, 1981

37
Shahak 153, Eitham air base, 1981

38
Shahak 107, Eitham air base, 1981

39
Nesher 666, Flight Test Centre, Tel Nof, late 1970s

29

This gallery section has been specially created by profile artist Mark Styling so as to better illustrate the colourful squadron and kill markings worn by the Shahaks and Neshers featured in profile. These drawings have been produced following exhaustive cross-referencing with published squadron histories, correspondence with surviving pilots and the detailed study of original photographs.

31

1

2

3

4

SIX DAY WAR

Soviet intelligence that Israel was concentrating forces along the Syrian border in the wake of the 7 April 1967 skirmish hardened Arab solidarity. The information was false, but Egypt expelled the UN observation force from Sinai, forward deployed ground forces into the resulting vacuum and imposed a blockade on Israeli Red Sea shipping and air traffic through the Straits of Tiran. Israel's regular army was unable to respond, and the mobilisation of reserves only resulted in further escalation, and a feeling that war was now inevitable. Jordan followed the Egyptian and Syrian lead by mobilising its troops in early June, at which point Israel decided to launch a pre-emptive strike, spearheaded by an IDF/AF attack on Egyptian air bases.

The objective was to win air superiority, thereby ensuring both the success of any Israeli ground offensive and the troops' protection against possible raids by Egyptian Tu-16 and Il-28 bombers. Spearheading the strike were the three Shahak squadrons. They were tasked with attacking the most distant and threatening targets, to defend Israel's airspace and to protect the less capable IDF/AF fighter-bombers.

The overwhelming surprise achieved by the Israeli strike on 5 June 1967 resulted in minor opposition compared with what might have been expected from the Arab air forces. During the first wave, which lasted between 0745 and 0900 hrs, the Shahaks were credited with six kills. Dan Sever was the first Shahak pilot to draw blood. He recalled;

'I was leading a three-ship formation, and our mission was to attack Bir Tamada air base with 500-kg bombs and then fly a CAP. We bombed the runway, and as we pulled out and flew north we saw pillars of black smoke coming from the nearby Bir Gafgafa air base. I looked in that direction and saw an Il-14 flying slowly at about 3000 ft. I reported it to my Nos 2 and 3 and then dived at it at full speed. When I was still several kilometres away I saw a MiG-21 turning east. I also reported this and readied my jet for the attack. Having closed to a range of 600 m, I was just about to squeeze the trigger when the MiG entered a spin. Two turns and it crashed. I told my pilots, "He crashed. We're returning to the Il-14",

Shahaks destroyed more aircraft on the ground then in the air during the Six Day War. Here, a No 101 Sqn aircraft strafes an Egyptian Tu-16 and Il-28 at Cairo West. Note that the Tupolev bomber in the foreground is armed with AS-1 air-to-surface missiles

Only a dozen Shahaks were left behind on alert as the complete IDF/AF combat aircraft fleet was launched in the pre-emptive strikes on Egyptian air bases on the morning of 5 June 1967

but we couldn't see the transport aircraft. It had disappeared.

'When we returned home the intelligence officer grabbed me and said, "Sever, do you know who was in that transport aircraft? It was flying the high command of the Egyptian Army, which was caught with its pants down. Gen Amer and his officers were visiting the front in Sinai. They were in that aircraft. You should have shot it down". It was a story that haunted me for years. A fighter pilot chases fighters, but in that particular case the right thing to do have done would have been to shoot down the transport aircraft.'

Each Shahak squadron left behind two pairs of aircraft on alert, and these were to be scrambled in the event of any retaliatory Arab air attacks. As this threat evaporated, and the element of surprise was no longer important, the alert Shahaks were scrambled to fly offensive CAPs in an effort to protect the attacking IDF/AF aircraft. One was led by David Ivry, with Ilan Gonen as his wingman. Ivry was one of the most experienced Shahak pilots at the time, having flown the delta-fighter since his conversion in France in 1961 and commanded No 117 Sqn between 1964-66. Gonen was one of least experienced, having joined the delta-fighter 'club' in 1965. Ilan Gonen recalled;

'We patrolled for a long time and there were no MiGs over Sinai. Then Ivry had a radio problem so the procedure was that I talked with the controller, and took the lead. We then intercepted an Il-14, so it turned out that I was the first to open fire. The Egyptian pilot acted properly. I hit his engine and it caught fire. The Il-14 was flying so low that the pilot immediately lowered the gear and landed straight ahead in the desert while it was burning. Ivry hit him while he was already on the ground.'

These first kills highlighted two controversial issues – should a pilot be credited with a kill if his victim crashed without a shot being fired, and how should shared claims be credited? Over the years quite a number of Arab fighters crashed while engaging Shahaks, either hitting the ground during low flying or spinning out of control, usually due to pilot error. At first the chasing pilot was declared responsible for the destruction of the enemy aircraft and credited with the kill, but in later years the attitude changed. Arab fighters lost in combat because of pilot error were credited to the squadron, and they became known as 'squadron kills'.

The first Six Day War kill was credited to Dan Sever in Shahak 77, which is seen here configured as a fighter-bomber

Israel was so desperate for aircraft on the opening morning of the Six Day War that it even armed the ex-Iraqi MiG-21 with two Shafrir 2 test AAMs and had it parked alongside the Shahaks that were manning the No 101 Sqn alert complex

The Il-14 shot down by Ilan Gonen sits forlornly on its undercarriage in the Sinai desert on 5 June 1967. Note that the transport's right wing has broken in two outboard of the engine, this damage being caused by a fire that was started by cannon shells shot from Gonen's Shahak 59

This gun camera still from a No 117 Sqn Shahak reveals that its pilot strafed two Egyptian Su-7s and an Il-28 during his attack on Fayid

The issue of sharing credit was even more complex, and was often the subject of heated debate. Again, the IDF/AF attitude changed over the years. Initially, the first pilot to hit the target was credited with the kill. Then it was considered that the one who had delivered the *coupe de grace* should receive the credit. Eventually, the preferred choice among commanders was for kills to be to shared whenever real ambiguity arose. There was also the issue of kills that remained unconfirmed, either by witnesses or camera-gun film. Such claims were usually dismissed, but as some air combats were closely monitored, there were cases when Intelligence was able to supply confirmation. Pilots called them 'Air4 kills', because Intelligence was the air department's fourth branch.

There was, however, no such debate over the four victories scored in the first wave of the attack by No 119 Sqn pilots Eitan Karmi and Giora Rom. They had been scrambled from Tel Nof to Abu Sueir air base, where Egyptian MiG-21s attempted to intercept IDF/AF attack aircraft. Each Shahak pilot was credited with two kills apiece.

A Day to Remember

The follow-up second wave completed the damage to Egyptian air power. The IDF/AF achieved the air superiority it sought and, although Egypt continued to operate aircraft until the last day of the war, its air force had been effectively neutralised.

After its successes in the first wave, No 119 Sqn was credited with the only kills to be claimed during the second. Four of the unit's Shahaks were briefed to attack the distant Ardaka air base on the Red Sea coast. By then the element of surprise no longer existed, and Ardaka, spared by the first wave, was now well prepared. A MiG-19 CAP was covering the approaches, but as the Shahaks raced in at the start of their bombing runs, the MiGs were too far away to intervene. And when they were finally able to attack, all four were lost. Ran Ronen was credited with two kills and Arnon Levoshin, who had only been flying the Shahak since December 1966, got his first. The fourth MiG-19 became the unit's first 'squadron kill', being destroyed as it attempted to land on the cratered runway.

By this time Jordan and Syria had joined the battle, Syrian MiG-17s, escorted by MiG-21s and Jordanian Hunters, streaking across the border bound for Israeli targets. The Shahaks responded with two simultaneous actions aimed at removing the new threat once and for all. Attack formations were ordered to attack Jordanian and Syrian air bases, while available Shahaks were scrambled to engage the intruders.

Oded Sagi of No 119 Sqn downed a Jordanian Hunter after he and his wingman had launched Shafrir AAMs which all missed. In fact, all but one of these missiles launched during the war missed their targets, and even the round which found its mark did not result in credit for a full kill.

SIX DAY WAR

35

This shot of Al-Minya air base was taken just moments after it had been bombed by Shahaks. The attacking aircraft flew their bombing pattern along the runway axis, the first pair dropping their ordnance a third of the way down the runway and the second pair delivering their bombs at the two-thirds point

The MiG-17 could be a dangerous enemy for it was highly manoeuvrable and able to withstand a lot of battle damage. The preferred Shahak tactic against 'inferior' fighters was 'stitching', using the vertical dimension rather than by starting a turning contest

With Nos 101 and 119 Sqns sharing 11 kills between them, it was now the turn of No 117 Sqn to clear Israel's northern airspace of Syrian and Lebanese intruders. In a series of engagements, the unit's pilots were credited with six kills for the loss of one Shahak. Amnon Arad shot down two Syrian MiG-17s, with a third credited to Ezra Dotan, and Ehud Henkin and Uri Gil each claimed a Syrian MiG-21, although Henkin had to eject as his Shahak was fatally damaged by debris from the explosion of the MiG-21 he had just destroyed. Finally, the squadron's acting CO, Uri Aven-Nir, downed a Lebanese Hunter.

While No 117 Sqn was hunting MiGs over northern Israel, a No 119 Sqn formation on a mission to attack T-4 air base engaged two defending Syrian MiG-21s and shot down both of them. The kills were credited to Giora Rom and Asher Snir.

From the afternoon of 5 June until war's end, No 117 Sqn Shahaks flew continuous daytime CAPs over Dmier air base in an effort to neutralise the remaining Syrian MiG-21s. They left Ramat David in the heaviest possible air-to-air configuration, with three external fuel tanks, and headed for Dmeir, crossing the Syrian border at about 15,000-16,000 ft. They continued to climb to 25,000 ft so as to stay above Syrian radar-guided 85 mm AAA, which was effective up to 22,000 ft. Such missions lasted up to 1 hrs 40 mins.

By the end of the day the magnitude of the Israeli victory could be fully appreciated. Roughly 75 percent of Egyptian air power had been destroyed, Syria had lost about half of its combat aircraft strength, the Jordanian air force was wiped-out and even Iraqi and Lebanese air power had been successfully engaged. The Shahak had proven its worth as a versatile fighting machine. It had borne the brunt of the initial air strikes, attacking the furthest and best-defended targets as well as protecting the less capable fighters and frustrating Arab intervention. The Shahak community was credited with 19 kills on 5 June, taking the total so far to 30. Ran Ronen was heading the list of MiG killers with four, ahead of Giora Rom with three. The emergence of the first Israeli Shahak ace was imminent.

FIVE MORE DAYS

Air-to-air action did not stop completely, and residual Arab air power continued to offer targets to the eager Shahak pilots. The first opportunity to engage Egyptian fighters arose early on 6 June when Su-7s were sent to attack Israeli ground forces in northern Sinai. In four successive engagements the Shahaks downed five Su-7s, with four of the kills credited to No 101 Sqn pilots Yitzhak Barzilai, Giora Epstein, Baruch Friedman and Avshalom Ran. The fifth went to No 119 Sqn EP Oded Sagi.

Shortly after the northern Sinai Su-7 hunt ceased, hectic action over Ramat David resulted in No 117 Sqn being credited with 2.5 kills. The engagement began as four Vautours and two Shahaks were preparing for an attack on the distant Iraqi H-3 air base. While Yehuda Koren was being briefed, the Vautours were already at the take-off point, waiting for him and his wingman, Pessach Shraga. He glanced outside and saw a large aircraft flying overhead, which he thought looked 'like a Boeing'. He recalled, 'It was painted silver overall, and flying in a right turn with its tail turret shooting. The bases's AAA sites returned fire, as the "Boeing" was actually a Tupolev'.

It was indeed an Iraqi Tu-16, and it was engaged not only by the local AAA but also by a pair of No 117 Sqn Shahaks. Amnon Arad hit the bomber with a Shafrir AAM, but the kill was shared by Arad and the AAA, possibly because the bomber crashed onto Megido barracks and killed 14 IDF troops. The Shahaks took-off as escorts for the Vautours on the H-3 raid minutes later. Koren thought it would be an easy mission, although;

'I was afraid we would not be able to locate the target. We followed the Vautours in line astern so that when they pulled up to attack we could climb and watch. We flew over Jabel Druz – wild landscape, desert. Here and there we observed three camels and a Bedouin. Where did they come from? Where they were going? When we passed over the Iraq-Jordan border we noticed an Iraqi division digging defensive positions, and I thought to myself "Why are they digging? Who would attack them?"

'When we got nearer, the Vautours accelerated, and I observed a spot ahead. At first I was not sure – was it a bird, or was it dirt on the windscreen? It looked like an aircraft. I informed the Vautours. We pulled-up and got closer. That spot was an aircraft, but I was closing too fast. I deployed the air brakes, switched off the afterburner and was still flying with external fuel tanks. It was a Hunter. I pulled-up in order not to pass him, but I was too fast and had to give up. We were on the downwind leg of the landing circuit. I decelerated to his speed – the speed of the circuit, which was very slow. We turned on base leg and then finals, and I could see that he was No 2 in the circuit. He was on finals and I was right on his tail, within cannon range.

'I looked to see if there was anyone behind me. I also looked up and I saw a Vautour with its bomb-bay doors open, shadowing me. I thought to myself "If I don't escape he will bomb me, so I quit my chase after the Hunter. The Vautour bombed the runway and the No 1 Hunter fell into one of the craters and exploded like napalm. My Hunter accelerated, retracted its undercarriage and raised its flaps. He had not yet seen me, and he commenced a climbing turn to the left. I was behind him, and when I checked my tail I heard, "No 1, break". I broke, but saw nothing. I jettisoned the external fuel tanks, opened the throttle and then understood that the No 1 being warned was the Vautour leader. They didn't use call-signs and we had no mutual briefing before the mission.

'I then saw the same Hunter flying east at 5000-6000ft. It wasn't flying fast because I closed on it very quickly. I squeezed the trigger and I could see hits and debris. I then had a compressor stall – too much hot gas from the cannon had entered the engine. The cure was to lower the nose, increase speed, let the aircraft "breathe" and then open the throttle. If there was no response then it was recommended to shut down the engine and re-start it. All this over H-3 at 5000-6000ft!

'I lowered the nose to increase speed but I didn't gain enough, so when I opened the throttle the

Giora Epstein shot down an Egyptian Su-7 in Shahak 56 on 6 June 1967, this being the first of his eventual 17 kills

Shahak 45 was a unique performer, shooting down a Lebanese Hunter on 5 June when flown by Uri Aven-Nir, followed by two Iraqi fighters the next day claimed by Yehuda Koren. Seated in front of the aircraft is Lt Gen Yitzhak Rabin, IDF/AF chief of staff 1964-68, who is seen here bidding farewell to the Ramat David 'warriors' in December 1967

engine didn't respond. I was now at about 3000-4000ft, and had just one more chance. If I wasn't successful I would have to eject. This time I gained more speed, and at the last moment I opened the throttle. The engine responded. I could breathe again.'

One of the Vautour pilots reported later that he saw the Hunter pilot eject. Based on that information, Koren was credited with his second kill. But the combat was not over yet, as Koren related;

'I then saw something gleaming. I looked back and saw a silver MiG-21 flying north behind me. I was flying east, more or less. I opened the throttle and looked left to see where he was. I saw a pair of Vautours pulling out of a strafing pass, with the MiG-21 following them. I shouted, "Vautours flying north. A MiG is right behind you. Break". Everyone heard me except those two, who turned out to be Moshe "Simi" Sa'ar and Ran Zur. The MiG pilot closed the distance but he didn't launch a missile or open fire. He actually did nothing.

'I wasn't in charge of the operation, but at that stage I had about 1700-1750-litres of fuel left. As our minimum for leaving the target area was 1650, I decided it was time to go home. I told everyone to disengage and head west. The two Vautours turned west and the MiG followed. I also turned west and went after it. Meanwhile, the MiG had entered a scissors manoeuvre with Zur. One act of scissors, then a second and I was closing. When he had finished the second I was at cannon range. A very short burst cut off its right wing and the MiG crashed immediately. Zur passed over him in his Vautour, thanking me on the radio at the same time.'

Sporadic Egyptian air activity over Sinai resulted in three engagements and six kills. The first involved two pairs of Shahaks, Guri Palter leading the jets from No 101 Sqn, with Giora Furman as his wingman. Meanwhile, Uri Ye'ari and wingman Ithamar Neuner led the No 119 Sqn pair, which was vectored to support the No 101 Sqn jets. Furman recalled;

'We patrolled over Tel Nof for quite some time before we were vectored towards Port Said, where we met the MiGs. As a result of a communication malfunction, Palter turned the other way. I shot down the first and then got worried about my low fuel state, but Uri Ye'ari came in and downed the other MiG. My kill was from 300 m without a radar lock. Immediately after the MiG was hit it just stopped in the air, and I had to avoid him. By then he was hanging on his parachute, and I had to worry about my fuel state.'

Further south over Jabel Mara, a pair of No 119 Sqn Shahaks flown by Oded Sagi and Omri Afek engaged four Egyptian MiG-19s. Each Shahak pilot was credited with a kill. Four hours later two No 101 Sqn Shahaks intercepted more MiG-19s over Jabel Mara, and this time Oded Marom and Uri Shachar claimed two apiece. But dwindling Arab air activity meant fewer prospects for engaging the enemy. This was especially true for No 117 Sqn, which focused its CAP activity over Syria, while Nos 101 and 119 Sqns patrolled Sinai, where Egyptian aircraft were still active.

Yehuda Koren's action on 6 June had indicated that if ever there was an opportunity for enemy aircraft to be engaged, it was over H-3. When another Vautour strike was planned for the morning of 7 June, No 117 Sqn's pilots were eager to escort the bombers on the mission. Due to the intense air opposition encountered on the previous day's raid, the number of escorting Shahaks was doubled to four – a decision which was

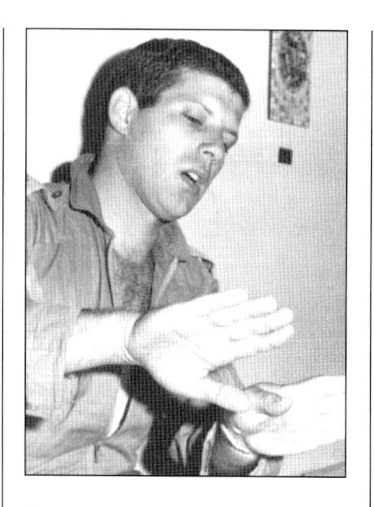

Oded Marom shot down a MiG-19 in Shahak 15 on 6 June 1967. It was a first for both the pilot and his aircraft

No 117 Sqn H-3 strike team (from left to right), Amnon Arad, Reuven Har'el, David Porat, Ezra 'Baban' Dotan, Shraga Pessach and Yehuda Koren. Gidon Dror is absent, having been shot down during the long range mission to Iraq

to handicap the delta-fighters. Mission planners thought that if four Shahaks were flying all the way to H-3, why not use them to carry bombs as well? Only after bombing were the Shahaks, flown by Ezra Dotan, Gideon Dror, David Porat and Reuven Har'el, to climb and protect the Vautours. But Dror recalled how carrying bombs had robbed them of their advantage;

'Instead of coming from above to protect the Vautours, we had to defend ourselves with no airspeed at low altitude. You can't give an aircraft two conflicting orders. Either it attacks or protects – it can't do both. We pulled to 5000 ft to look for the target, and this probably alarmed all the radars in the area. We lost the element of surprise. They waited for us, the ground below burning from the AAA fire, and there were also fighters in the air. I bombed and then saw two Hunters chase the other pair. I closed on one of them and shot it down, but I was then hit myself. I rolled to the right and the stick wasn't responding. When I saw the ground getting closer I ejected. It was really low – I was only three or four seconds in the air. I buried my maps and then a jeep arrived with Iraqi soldiers.'

Gideon Dror became a prisoner of war in Iraq. He returned to Israel on 26 June 1967 after 19 days in captivity. Although Dotan was also credited with a kill over H-3, the fact that two of the Vautours were also shot down resulted in an unfavourable kill to loss ratio of 2-to-3.

On the third day of the war, Sinai air activity was concentrated over the southern section of the frontline as advancing Israeli troops completed the peninsula's capture. A No 101 Sqn formation was scheduled to take-off at 1430 hrs to attack Cairo West, where two Algerian MiG squadrons had just deployed in support of the Egyptians. However, before take-off the mission was changed to an interdiction along the Sharem El-Sheikh to A-Tur road. Amos Amir led Baruch Friedman, Uri Shachar and Yochai Richter, but the formation's target was again changed, as Amir recalled;

'Close to the Gulf of Suez, the controller informed us that there were MiGs in the area, so we intercepted them. By then I was quite worried because everybody had downed a MiG, yet I hadn't even seen one in the air. It was very frustrating. It was a four-ship formation of MiG-19s, and I don't know what they were doing there. Maybe they were on a patrol. It was a simple combat, for the MiG-19 was both an inferior aircraft and a bad fighter. We came in behind their tails and shot two of them down. Another one entered a spin and crashed – maybe he panicked.'

Some three hours later history was made when the No 119 Sqn three-ship formation of Mordechai Yeshurun (leading), Giora Rom and Avraham Salmon was vectored onto MiG-17s that were attacking Israeli Super Mysteres in the Bir Gafgafa area. Rom shot down two to become not only the first Shahak ace, but also the first true IDF/AF one.

During the 1948 Israeli Independence War, Rudy Augarten had been credited with four kills, which were were added to the two victories (both

CHAPTER TWO

Amos Amir shot down an Egyptian MiG-19 in Shahak 09 on 7 June 1967

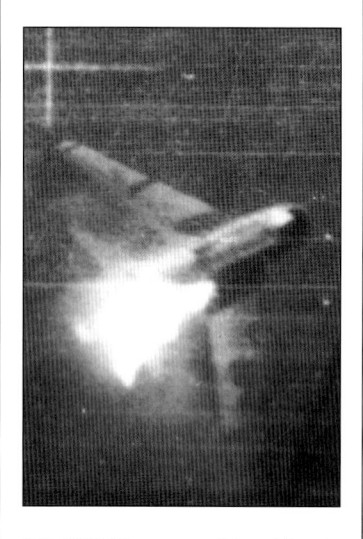

This MiG-19 was one of ten claimed as destroyed by Shahak pilots in aerial combat during the Six Day War. Possessing neither the agility of the MiG-17 or the speed of the MiG-21, the MiG-19 was viewed as an easy kill for any self-respecting Shahak pilot

The tail section of Ezra Dotan's Shahak 29 is seen after he carried out an emergency landing at Megiddo with damage inflicted by a Syrian AA-2 Atoll infra-red missile fired from a MiG-21

Messerschmitt Bf 109s) he had scored flying P-47Ds with the USAAF's 403rd Fighter Group in Europe during World War 2 to make him an ace. Rom, however, was the first Israeli pilot to be credited with five kills in IDF/AF service.

By the end of the war's third day, the Shahak pilots had 39.5 kills and the IDF/AF's first ace had been acclaimed. Others were close behind – Ronen had four kills and Dotan, Koren and Sagi each had three. Another 28 pilots shared 34.5 victories between them, and the final two were 'squadron kills'. Of the 31 pilots who had scored so far, 15 were to become aces.

Activity over Sinai on the fourth day followed the pattern set over the preceding two, with limited Egyptian air operations and few engagements, although two separate encounters between opposing fighters over Romani resulted in four more kills for the Israelis. Arlozor Lev was credited with a MiG-17, while No 119 Sqn pilots Avraham Salmon and Menachem Shmul got two and one MiG-19s respectively. That afternoon, over the same area, three successive engagements resulted in four kills, but at the cost of a Shahak. Yossi Arazi recalled;

'At first we "ironed" the skies west of Be'er Sheba. Suddenly, we heard Salmon reporting that Il-28s were crossing the Sinai coast near Bardavil. We rushed to that area but found nothing. We climbed, and were already low on fuel, when the controller called me. "MiGs are attacking our troops at Kantara, go there". We flew to Kantara and patrolled at low altitude. With only 1200 litres of fuel left – the minimum for a safe return to base from that area – I was about to order my wingman Maoz Poraz to return to base when I saw explosions on the ground, then a MiG-21. I then saw four Egyptian MiG-21s and four dark-painted MiG-17s, which I think were Algerian. We had intelligence information that Algeria was sending MiG-17s to Egypt, and these aircraft were painted differently.

Yossi Arazi shot down a MiG-21 in Shahak 15 on 8 June 1967. It was the pilot's first kill and the aircraft's second

'Two things crossed my mind. The first was, "What the hell was going on? In this war *we* attacked, so why did they attack our troops? These were not the rules of the game!" Then I thought about Avner Slapak. He was the best pilot in the squadron. I thought to myself, "How could I return to the squadron and tell Slapak that I had seen eight MiGs and didn't even shoot down one of them, no matter what my fuel state was?"

'We were still flying with empty 1300-litre external fuel tanks, so I ordered them to be jettisoned. We were at low altitude at high speed – over 500 knots – and the jettisoning rocked the aircraft so violently that the 'chute on which I was sitting slipped forward between my knees. I sank in the seat. My knees were now in such a position that I couldn't reach the pedals, nor see anything behind me. In such a state I entered combat! I caught a MiG-21, but then saw another on my tail, launching air-to-ground rockets at me. I broke. I ordered Maoz to engage him, and he chased him south towards Ismailiya. I was left alone with seven MiGs. I tried to follow a MiG-17, but suddenly I passed a MiG-21 and entered a scissors manoeuvre with him. We were so low that I looked at the shadow of my jet on the ground. If I saw another shadow I broke away.

'I broke two or three times until a MiG-21 simply flew into my sight, asking for a cannon burst. I opened fire, but I was probably a bit excited and my aim wasn't good. I then remembered Aryeh Ben-Or. He engaged MiGs before the war, but failed to shoot them down, and when he returned he said, "To shoot down a MiG you have to be super-persistent, they don't fall by themselves". So I organised my gunsight and squeezed the trigger until the MiG exploded. I didn't see an ejection.

'The MiG-21 had its oxygen bottle very close to a high-octane fuel tank, and they made an interesting pyrotechnic display and a very impressive explosion. I then observed another MiG at a range of 600 m, but at a pretty high deflection angle. It was far from ideal, but I had no more fuel so I opened fire. I exhausted my ammunition but didn't get a hit.

'When we entered combat it was clear that I wouldn't be able to return to Hatzor, but I ordered Maoz to disengage at 600 litres and go for an emergency landing at El-Arish. After I'd shot at the second MiG, I escaped at low altitude. I had no ammunition and no fuel, and there

The Shahak pilots quickly discovered that the MiG-21 usually burst into flames when hit by 30 mm cannon shells

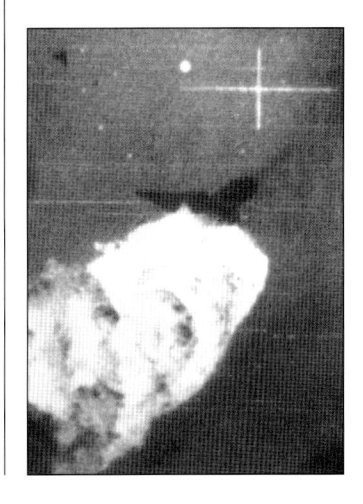

were still six MiGs out there. I flew for a minute at low altitude and then climbed to plan my landing at El-Arish. Then Maoz informed me that he had no fuel left and was planning to land on the Kantara to El-Arish road. I ordered him to eject, which he did.

'I was at high altitude and saw both El-Arish and Hatzerim. I had 200 litres left, and I thought that if I landed at El-Arish it would take three days to recover the aircraft, so I opted for Hatzerim. I landed with barely 70 litres of fuel in the tanks. And who do I meet there but my good friend Aryeh Ben-Or? I told him about the combat while my aircraft was refuelled and then I returned to Hatzor. Beni Peled was the base commander, and when I returned he welcomed me and said "Well done, but f..." – "Well done" for the kill, and "f..." because my wingman had ejected.'

Avraham Salmon was flying Shahak 55 when he transmitted the report which actually vectored the No 101 Sqn pair, led by Arazi, towards the northern coast of Sinai. Shahak 55 was considered to be a jinxed aircraft. Men who operate machines tend to humanise them, so that while the Shahaks may have all looked similar, to the pilots, each was thought to have its own distinctive qualities – some were faster, some were more powerful and others had better harmonised guns, but Shahak 55 was the one with the worst reputation. Its cannon had jammed at least three times in combat with a MiG centred in the gunsight. Worse, it had crashed twice, seriously injuring two pilots. On the other hand, Shahak 58, flown by Salmon's wingman Reuven Rozen was a real beauty. It was not only credited with 12 kills, but all seven of the pilots who scored victories while flying it became aces. Rozen recalled;

'We fought two MiG-17s and they were good, aggressive pilots flying a manoeuvrable platform. I turned with one of them and he managed to come within range to open fire right behind me. The MiG-17 wasn't equipped with AAMs, so I simply levelled my wings and accelerated out of his cannon range. I then climbed and returned for another round. The best pilot in that air combat was Salmon. He could downed both of them, but he was flying Shahak 55 and his cannon jammed. At a certain stage in that combat the MiGs flew line astern roughly 800 m apart. Salmon then made another attempt, but for some reason he selected the first MiG-17. He was in a sandwich – a dangerous situation. This helped me achieve my kill because Salmon was flying 200 m behind their leader and 500 m in front of the trailing MiG, which concentrated on Salmon instead of me. It was my opportunity, and I opened fire, hitting the right wing. But he kept flying. I didn't even claim a kill because I didn't see it crash. Intelligence later reported that the MiG had crashed, however – an Air4 kill.

'When I pulled-up from that MiG I saw an Il-28 flying east

No 101 Sqn pilots gathered for a photograph shortly after the war had ended. They are, standing (from left to right), Arlozor Lev, Amos Lapidot (CO), Michael Haber, Avner Slapak, Dan Sever (senior deputy CO), Yoram Agmon, Ezra Aharon, Guri Palter, Ron Holdai, Eldad Palter and Amnon Shamir. Sitting (from left to right) are Yiftach Spector (junior deputy CO), Yitzhak Barzilai, Yossi Arazi, Giora Furman (Hatzor OC Flying), Yak Nevo (Hatzor air base commander), Eldad Ran, Eli Zohar, Amnon Shadmi and Giora Epstein. These 20 pilots had a cumulative score of 14.5 kills by the end of the Six Day War, including three credited to Mystere pilot Nevo

towards Egypt. I was pretty inexperienced then. In training, I was used to a certain size of aircraft to estimate the range. I never practiced with bombers or transports, so I opened fire at 700 m and had no chance of scoring because I treated it as if it was a MiG. I should have got much closer. It was lack of experience, lack of practice and something else – he was shooting back at me! The rear gunner returned fire, which was a surprise, for aircraft didn't usually shoot back at us. Once again my cannon had a deflection to the right, and its right engine caught fire. Intelligence reported that it landed 50 minutes later at Cairo West on one engine.'

Another No 119 Sqn pair operating in the area at the time was more successful in engaging the Il-28s. Ya'acov Agassi and his wingman Menachem Shmul intercepted three, and Shmul shot down one of the bombers. The pair turned west to look for the others, but were engaged by four MiG-21s. Shmul also shot one of these down as well.

Activity over Sinai declined as IDF ground forces completed the occupation, and air combats had become rare by 9 June when the final three Shahak kills of the war were claimed. A No 119 Sqn pair, led by Snir, with his wingman Ilan Hait flying the notorious No 55, intercepted Egyptian MiG-17s attacking Israeli ground forces in northern Sinai. Snir shot down both, with Hait joining the list of frustrated fighter pilots who engaged the enemy in Shahak 55, only to have its cannon jam. Then the IDF focus turned north to the Golan Heights, where the Israeli offensive may have prompted a Syrian attempt to launch fighters. The fortunate No 117 Sqn pilot flying CAP over Dmier was Ehud Henkin, who was credited with a MiG-21 kill.

The next day a cease-fire came into effect. Israel occupied the Sinai Peninsula, the West Bank and the Golan Heights, having shattered the Egyptian, Jordanian and Syrian armies. Shahak pilots were credited with 50.5 kills for the loss of four aircraft, while another five fell to AAA and SAMs. Although quite a number of Shafrirs were launched during the conflict, the performance of the Israeli infra-red AAM was far from satisfactory, leaving the cannon to reign supreme. Of the Shahak kills, 28 per cent were credited to four pilots, including the first Shahak ace, Giora Rom. He would soon share his elite status with two other pilots.

No 117 Sqn pilots also posed for a group shot, this time with Shahak 64, at war's end. Sat on the fuselage are (from left to right) Yossi Henkin, Shlomo Navot (in cockpit), Amichai Roke'ach, Amnon Gardi, Yuval Ne'eman, Amit Livni, Amos Cohen, Uri Dekel and Uri Liss, whilst on the wing (from left to right) are Adi Benaya, Shraga Pessach, Shabtai Gilboa (Ramat David OC Flying) and the squadron Intelligence Officer. Finally, standing (from left to right), are Yiftach Zemmer (junior deputy CO), Ezra Dotan, David Porat, Amnon Halivni, Avraham Oren, Uri Gil, Yehezkel Somech (Ramat David air base CO), Meir Livneh, Dror Avneri, Amichai Shamueli (CO), Uri Aven-Nir (senior deputy CO), Amnon Arad, Yehuda Koren, Reuven Har'el, Avi Lanir, the squadron navigator, Shlomo Nir, Naftali Porat and Ehud Henkin

ATTRITION

There were no diplomatic efforts to ease the tension in the Middle East after the clear-cut Israeli victory in the Six Day War. Quite the contrary, in fact. Egypt's President Abdel Gamal El-Nasser declared 'what has been taken by force will be returned by force'. In September 1967 Arab leaders adopted the 'three-no' policy at the Khartoum Summit – no recognition, no negotiation and no peace with Israel.

In the light of this diplomatic dead-end, hostilities continued on a limited scale after the war. The rehabilitation of Egyptian and Syrian military power commenced immediately, however, fuelled by generous aid from the USSR. The Soviet leadership was worried about the Cold War implications of the defeat of Arab forces, using their hardware and doctrine, by a tiny nation equipped with Western weapons.

The relatively small number of casualties suffered by Egyptian and Syrian personnel during the conflict, coupled with the massive Soviet arms build-up, returned those countries' air forces to pre-June 1967 equipment levels within a few months. Lessons learned were also implemented. For example, Arab air bases were 'hardened' to protect aircraft from air strikes and reduce the vulnerability of dispersal sites. More significantly, Arab air force chiefs realised that their fighter pilots were no match for the Shahaks when employing Soviet tactics in Soviet aircraft.

The Egyptian and Syrian response to Israeli air superiority came, therefore, not in the air but on the ground. In 1968 the Egyptian Air Defence Force (ADF) was formed to assume responsibility for protecting the country's airspace. With the creation of a network of SAM sites, overlapping in coverage, protected by AAA and supported by control centres, radar stations and MiG-21s, it was set to challenge Israeli air superiority.

ACES AND MISSILES

Despite these changes, six aerial engagements in July 1967 resulted in a further six Israeli kills. On 8 July No 119 Sqn senior deputy CO Avihu Ben-Nun shot down an Egyptian MiG-21. A week later, on the 15th, history was made when the unit's CO, Ran Ronen, shot down an Egyptian MiG-21 with a Shafrir missile. This was not the first kill by an AAM in the history of Middle East air warfare, nor was it the first by an infra-red

Ran Ronen was the first Israeli pilot to be credited with a kill – a MiG-21 on 15 July 1967 – using the indigenous Shafrir AAM

Shahak 83 displays a single victory marking after the first Shafrir kill on 15 July 1967

Refidim was the ex-Egyptian airfield Bir Gafgafa, and it served as the hub of IDF/AF activity in Sinai following its capture in June 1967. The wreckage of two Mi-6 helicopters can be seen on either side of the parallel taxyway. They had been destroyed on the ground on 5 June 1967, their charred remains being unceremoniously bulldozed out of the way in order to render the base operational once again. Runway 15/33 can be seen on the left

missile, as an Egyptian MiG-21 had downed a Shahak with an AA-2 Atoll on 5 June 1967. Nevertheless, it was the first in a long list of successes for the Rafael family of IR AAMs. It also signalled a revolution in air warfare because the IR AAM would now gradually take-over from the cannon as the principle aerial weapon.

Doubling his score, Ronen became Israel's second ace. He was closely followed by Asher Snir, who was credited with two Egyptian MiG-17s later that same day. Interestingly, the first three Israeli aces were all No 119 Sqn pilots. Two more kills, on 15 July, were credited to Eliezer Prigat and Yoram Agmon, who claimed a MiG-21 and an Su-7 respectively.

The July engagements were followed by a period of relative inactivity until early 1969. There was, however, occasional fighting on land and at sea while both sides prepared for a renewal of hostilities.

To improve the protection of Israeli troops in Sinai, a Shahak alert detachment was established on 26 July 1967 at Refidim (the Israeli name for the former Egyptian base of Bir Gafgafa, in central Sinai) by a No 101 Sqn four-ship formation led by acting CO, Dan Sever. Responsibility for manning the detachment was shared by all three Shahak squadrons on a rotational basis, with a change being made every two weeks.

During its period of duty the squadron's pilots were also rotated, crews being changed every few days so that everyone shared the burden. Many kills achieved by the delta-fighters between 1969 and 1973 were claimed by the Refidim alert jets. As a result, pilots were eager to be sent there during times of particular tension for the probability of an air engagement was high, thus improving their chances of achieving a victory.

The first kill by a Refidim pilot was scored by Avihu Ben-Nun on 10 October 1967. He was leading a pair of Shahaks scrambled from the base to intercept four Egyptian MiG-21s which had penetrated Israeli airspace at dusk. Ben-Nun launched a Shafrir at the leading MiG but it missed, so he shot down the wingman with cannon fire.

The last Shahak delivered to Israel was Mirage IIIBJ 89, which was ferried from France by Danny Shapira and Avihu Ben-Nun on 17-18 January 1968. Two-seaters flew combat missions alongside single-seat Shahaks, 89 achieving two kills during the Yom Kippur War

A further kill was credited to the Shahaks in 1968 when No 101 Sqn CO Oded Marom downed an Egyptian MiG-17 on 10 December.

Although only a single kill was claimed by the Shahaks in 1968, it was still a significant year for the delta-fighter community for it saw the service introduction of the A-4 Skyhawk attack aircraft. This in turn meant that the Shahak could at last revert to being purely an air-to-air platform. From then on its pilots were to become known as the 'princes' of the skies within the IDF/AF, for although the 'mud-mover' attack pilots flew the most dangerous missions, yet were hardly recognised, the fighter 'princes' flew a relatively safe mission, yet captured public attention.

February 1969 focused activity on the Syrian border, and three more pilots joined the Shahak 'MiG killers' club. On the 12th Uri Liss shot down a Syrian MiG-21 with a Shafrir, while Amnon Shamir and Kobi Richter were each credited with single victories on the 24th.

ARTILLERY, SNIPERS AND COMMANDO RAIDS

Further south, the Egyptians had concluded that their armed forces were ready to resume hostilities, although they had correctly analysed the limitations of their power. Its larger regular army was able to sustain a long and costly static war, during which its advantages could be exploited to the full. These were the ability to use massive artillery fire, pin-point sniper action and limited-scale commando assaults. The resulting 17-month long Attrition War was formally launched on 8 March 1969 with Egyptian artillery shelling along the Suez Canal. It ended on 7 August 1970 with a US-brokered cease-fire agreement.

No 101 Sqn senior deputy CO Dan Sever inaugurated the Refidim alert on 26 July 1967 in Shahak 12

IDF/AF involvement in the war's first phase, between March and July 1969, was limited, units only reacting to Egyptian activity in an effort

to avoid an escalation in the conflict. Shahaks supported attack aircraft pounding Egyptian targets, as well as protecting ground units in Sinai from retaliatory air raids. The two kills credited to Shahak pilots in March and April 1969 were both achieved following a scramble from Refidim.

On 8 March 1969, No 101 Sqn pilots Giora Yoeli (leader) and Michael Zuk intercepted four Egyptian MiG-21s. Zuk entered a scissors manoeuvre with a MiG and Yoeli followed, enabling his wingman to recover energy and pull-up. Yoeli opened fire and damaged the MiG-21's wing before Zuk dived from above and hit the enemy fighter with a burst from his cannon. The MiG-21 exploded, and its pilot, Muhamad Abed El-Baki Ahmed Hassan, ejected. Quickly captured, the Egyptian pilot told his Israeli interrogators that he was engaged in an air combat with a Mirage when he was hit and his engine cut. While he was trying to re-start it, his MiG-21 was hit by a second burst of cannon fire and he ejected. Zuk was credited with the kill, which was his first victory.

The first kill for Michael Zuk and Shahak 14 was achieved on 8 March 1969 when he claimed an Egyptian MiG-21 – the first of his seven victories. Zuk died on 3 December 1975 in a Kfir accident

This latest conflict saw the debut of a new AAM in IDF/AF service, the American AIM-9B Sidewinder IR weapon being successfully employed by Shahak pilots. A total of 60 missiles had been purchased as part of the first Israeli F-4 Phantom II contract, and these were used pending availability of the improved Rafael Shafrir 2. Captured Soviet AA-2 missiles were also used by the Shahaks during the Attrition War, nine AA-2 launchers and several dozen missiles having been captured at Bir Gafgafa in June 1967. Testing soon revealed their compatibility with the Shahak, and they entered service with No 119 Sqn in December 1967.

Overall, the AA-2 was found to be comparable to the AIM-9B, and both weapons were considered superior to the Shafrir. They were, however, inferior to the Shafrir 2, which was due to enter service in mid-1969, and to the AIM-9D, scheduled to become operational in early 1970 – 250 examples of the latter were ordered as part of the Israeli F-4 purchase.

The first Shahak AIM-9B kill came on 14 April 1969 when a No 119 Sqn pair, led by Reuven Rozen, was scrambled from Refidim to intercept a decoy – Egyptian fighters simulating an air strike to distract Israeli attention from an Egyptian MiG-21 reconnaissance mission. Rozen admitted later that he had made a lot of errors in that combat;

A number of Soviet-made Egyptian AA-2 Atoll AAMs were seized at Bir Gafgafa in June 1967, and these were pressed into service with the IDF/AF in early 1968 following a successful test firing the previous November when Asher Snir launched four from a Shahak

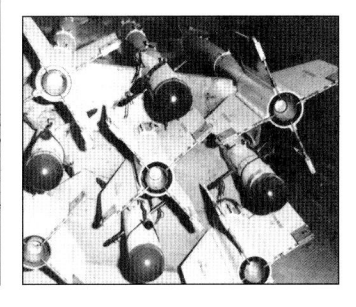

'I was not good, yet I was credited with a kill – sometimes the end result can tell you nothing about what really happened. We were scrambled from Refidim to intercept two four-ship formations. My first mistake was that I forgot to jettison the underbelly fuel tank. Although I was the leader, and did not order the external tanks to be jettisoned, my wingman, Menachem Eyal, remembered to do so. The combat started and I noticed everybody was faster than me. To fight a pair versus two four-ship formations with the additional drag of the underbelly fuel tank was a disaster. A MiG was soon on my tail.

'I saw it and did a high-speed yo-yo. Because of the tank, I had no chance to do it properly. But I was lucky since my opponent was not very good, so we entered a scissors. I could not perform this manoeuvre very well either because of the drag of the tank, but it was an error in any case to try it in a multi-bogey engagement when you had to maintain speed to preserve a high-energy state. Quite surprisingly I had the upper hand. I then considered trying a "Baharav Burst" (an off-bore-sight burst often used by IDF/AF ace Israel Baharav), but just as I was about to open fire he gave up. He dropped his nose and so did I, but because of the external fuel tank my acceleration wasn't as good. The range opened to 1200 m in no time at all, so I launched an AIM-9B. It exploded, but a complete aircraft emerged – I saw a red fireball, then black smoke and finally the MiG-21.

'Menachem Eyal was by my side, and I delayed the AAM launch to let him clear my field of fire. He chased a MiG-21, opening fire but without positive results. Then I warned him that a second MiG was on his tail and he broke away. Just then he saw a MiG-21 crashing. At that stage I made a serious error, for after I launched the AAM I waited to see the result.

'I should have expected somebody on my tail, and indeed there was a MiG right behind me. I was hit by two AAMs. One exploded under my belly and the other behind my tail – 200 fragments hit my aircraft. I broke so that the MiG which had launched the AAMs could not shoot me with his cannon. My aircraft was still responding so I disengaged. I was full of holes, but again I was lucky. None of the fragments had hit a vital system, although a gyro unit from one of the missiles got stuck in my vertical stabiliser, and I had a tiny oil leak. In the Shahak engine oil was critical. A warning light came on when I was downwind to land at Refidim. I landed safely. Two minutes more and I would have had a problem.'

After the mission was debriefed Rozen was credited with his second kill, but it had been a close call. On 21 May he got his third MiG-21;

'Ran Ronen was the CO and I was the squadron's reconnaissance officer. We planned to fly a recce mission to photograph a target near Luxor, so the day prior to the mission Ran came to see me at Tel Nof to prepare – No 119 Sqn were not on alert at Tel Nof, our squadron instead manning the alert at Refidim, and No 101 Sqn being on alert at Tel Nof. When Ran arrived, he asked the squadron's technical officer, "Do you have aircraft?" and the TO curtly answered, "We're not on alert". Ran then asked, "Do you have serviceable aircraft?", to which the TO replied "Yes". Ran ordered, "Prepare the fastest aircraft you can and report to me". When the TO reported that he had a pair of Shahaks on alert, Ran told me to put on my G-suit, and then called Rafi Harlev (Head of Air3, Operations Branch). "Rafi, I am on alert with Rozen. If you have something we are here". We then continued to draw up our maps for the recce mission.

No 119 Sqn CO Ran Ronen briefs his pilots on 3 March 1968

It wasn't long before we got a call from Rafi. "Ran, take Rozen and fly to Bardavil at low altitude. Maintain radio silence and wait for the call".

'So we flew low over Bardavil. We were then ordered to "Full power, 240, 20,000 ft, engage". Asher Snir and Eli Menachem had been scrambled from Refidim, and they had already engaged the enemy when we were vectored to help them. Ran turned onto a 240-degree heading and lifted the nose. We had difficulty jettisoning our external fuel tanks, for you had to be flying at precisely 350 knots with the nose lifted, and no loading on the wings, otherwise the seeker heads of the AAMs would fall off with the shock of the tanks coming away. So he did it just fine and he ordered, "Full power, ready to jettison external fuel tanks, jettison external fuel tanks!" Suddenly, I saw his AAMs launched straight ahead. I was amazed! He said nothing on the radio. Ran then pushed the *right* switch and jettisoned the external fuel tanks.

'The MiGs came at us in pairs in line astern. Ran turned after the first. I saw that if I followed him I would be directly in front of the next pair, so we separated. The next time I saw him was when we came in to land. :kidscdk) I chased an aircraft that wasn't aggressive and probably wanted to disengage. I closed on him, trading degrees for speed, but suddenly he levelled his wings and fled. I saw a tiny dot disappearing. Then I couldn't see anything, not a single aircraft. I felt terrible. Over the radio I could hear Ran, Asher and Eli fighting, but I could see nothing. I switched off my afterburner, as there was no point in burning fuel for nothing. I was frustrated, since in air combat you have three minutes before you loose your opportunity. I was flying northwest at 18,000 ft when I saw a MiG heading west at 4000 ft. I dropped my nose, but then I heard, "Stop the combat. Disengage". Now, after seeing an aircraft at last? No way!

'My MiG stopped manoeuvring and stabilised in a left turn at a range of 500 m, which was very convenient for me. At that stage I saw that I was overtaking a Shahak which I hadn't seen before. I passed him and heard Snir on the radio. Snir was sure it was Eli Menachem who was stealing his MiG, so he shouted, "No 2, a MiG on your tail. Break!" But I understood what he was up to. I didn't break, but Eli Menachem lost an opportunity for a kill. He was chasing a MiG when he heard Snir's warning so he broke. I opened fire and got a hit – nice kill. Then I disengaged.'

Ronen and Snir were each credited with a single MiG-21 kill, boosting their scores to six apiece. Eight days later Ithamar Neuner shot down a Syrian MiG-21 with a Shafrir, which proved to be the third, and last, kill credited to the Israel's first AAM. Shortly afterwards No 117 Sqn became the first Shahak unit to be equipped with the improved Shafrir 2.

Egyptian activity along the Suez Canal intensified as summer approached, and to avoid a further escalation in the conflict the IDF/AF launched a series of missions in June 1969 designed to deter the enemy through a demonstration of force. Known as Operation *Rimonim* (Pomegranates), aircraft patrolled south of Suez City in an area not covered by the Egyptian ADF. The Shahak pilots called it 'Texas', and small formations of experienced 'MiG killers' engaged the defending MiG-21s.

Between 24 June and 7 July nine Egyptian MiG-21s were shot down. Oded Marom and Yiftach Spector of No 101 Sqn improved their scores to three and 2.5 respectively, while Avinoam Keldes got his first kill. Meanwhile, No 119 Sqn's Asher Snir, Eitan Karmi and Amos Amir took their totals to seven, four and three respectively, and No 117 Sqn's Kobi Richter got his second. The latter was perhaps the most significant of the *Rimonim* kills as it was the first to be claimed with a Shafrir 2 AAM. Although the new missile was still being tested, Richter's success saw it duly declared operational.

Rimonim was a tremendous victory for the Shahak pilots, although it had no significant impact on the war. While it had taken them a fortnight to shoot down nine Egyptian MiG-21s, a single day's action on 8 July 1969 resulted in the destruction of seven Syrian MiG-21s. Three of the kills were attributed to Shafrir 2s, which meant that for the first time in the history of air warfare in the Middle East, the number of AAM kills in a multi-aircraft engagement almost equalled that scored with cannon.

Furthermore, since the Shafrir 2 was only available to No 117 Sqn, the result was even more astonishing, for 75 per cent of the kills claimed by the unit were credited to the Shafrir 2. Perhaps more than any other single air combat, this engagement represented a watershed in modern air warfare because of the shift in importance from cannon to IR AAMs. The seven kills were shared between No 117 Sqn's Uri Aven-Nir, Ran Goren, Shlomo Navot and Kobi Richter and No 101 Sqn's Eitan Ben-Eliyahu and Giora Furman. The latter was the only one credited with a two kills that day, one of which was a rare radar lock victory, as he explained;

'Pilots usually got excited when they entered air combat with a fluctuating radar lock, so there were switches on the stick that fixed the ranges and, indeed, most of the kills were from short range. Mine was achieved with a solid radar lock from 400-500 m – a classic. We used my gunsight film for years to explain to pilots that a kill with a radar lock was indeed possible.'

No 119 Sqn pilots are seen outside their HQ building at Tel Nof in January 1968. They are, standing (from left to right), Avihu Ben-Nun (senior deputy CO), Yitzhak Golan, Uri Ye'ari, Ran Ronen (squadron CO), Ilan Hait, Reuven Rozen and Eitan Karmi (junior deputy CO), and sitting (from left to right), Asher Snir, Baruch Keinan, Shlomo Egozi, Arnon Levoshin, Omri Afek and Yitzhak Nir

No 101 Sqn pilots preferred the AIM-9 AAM because of its elegant shape and smoother trajectory in comparison with the Shafrir 2, which spiralled its way to the target. Eitan Ben-Eliyahu scored Shahak 33's third kill on 8 July 1969

Operation BOXER

By the time man first set foot on the Moon, the Shahak community had registered 94.5 kills, with three aces being credited with 19 per cent of this total. Since the beginning of 1969, Egypt and Syria had lost 24 MiG-21s and a single MiG-17 in combat with Shahaks. The impact of these kills on the morale of Arab pilots should not be underestimated, but the cumulative effect of Egyptian artillery shelling, commando raids and sniping served to undermine Israeli achievements in the air. A much bigger demonstration of air power was required to deter Egypt from its continued war of attrition.

Israel took advantage of the world's preoccupation with the *Apollo* astronauts' triumph and launched Operation *Boxer* – an air offensive along the Suez Canal. Although greater use of air power was viewed as an escalation in an otherwise static war, Israeli decision-makers could not accept that Egypt was winning the conflict, and hoped that a demonstration of IDF/AF superiority would force a cease-fire. However, the Egyptian leadership had already lost face to Israeli air power in 1967, and it was impossible for them to back down now. Therefore, the *Boxer* offensive, launched on 20 July, did indeed lead to an escalation in the fighting.

Boxer lasted until 28 July, and resulted in an unsatisfactory Israeli air-to-air kill to loss ratio of 6-to-2, as well as a so-called 'friendly fire' incident on 25 July in which a No 101 Sqn Shahak damaged a No 119 Sqn jet. Three kills were credited to Shahaks on the first day of the offensive at the cost of two lost in combat with Egyptian MiG-21s. No 101 Sqn experienced both failure and success, and it also celebrated the emergence of its first ace, albeit an aircraft rather than a pilot. Yiftach Spector improved his score to 3.5 kills and Giora Epstein got his second, but it was Giora Yoeli's first victory which gave Shahak 59 its fifth kill, as he explained;

'We were two pairs in that air combat, and we were scrambled to intercept attacking Egyptian fighters. We located them when we observed the explosions of their bombs, and we entered air combat with the MiG-17s at low altitude. I quickly latched onto the tail of one of them, but the pilot turned his jet very well at low altitude – it was his advantage. We fought for at least two minutes, turning at low altitude all that time. I slowly closed on him, and the "G" force was so high that he must have eased off a little on the stick. At exactly that moment I opened fire with a long, crazy cannon burst. I saw part of his right wing fly away and he rolled straight down into the ground.'

Four days later a similar pattern emerged when Shahaks shot down a single MiG-21 and two Su-7s. Shlomo Navot of No 117 Sqn got the MiG (the fifth attributed to the Shafrir 2) and No 101 Sqn's Shamuel Gordon and Michael Zuk shared the Su-7s between them. Strangely enough, many Shahak pilots remember the MiGs they missed more clearly than the ones they shot down, which highlights their desire to learn and improve their performance through the analysis of their errors. On 24 July No 119 Sqn pair Yossi Henkin (leader) and Yitzhak Nir were vectored to the aid of No 117 Sqn Shahaks fighting Egyptian MiG-21s. Unlike most aircraft then in the frontline, Nir's Shahak 19 had already been painted in the soon-to-be standard IDF/AF post-Six Day War camouflage scheme. It was Nir's second air combat;

'Two No 117 Sqn pairs were engaging six or eight MiG-21s, and they soon called for help. The controller vectored us to the area, but Henkin didn't hear him. The controller screamed that No 117 Sqn was in trouble. I overtook him, waved my wings and jettisoned the external fuel tanks to get him to

Shahak 53 crashed in 1963, but was rebuilt by IAI as a result of the 1967 French embargo on the supply of further Mirage IIIs. Seen here taxiing in October 1968, the aircraft still boasts its red and white striped rudder from when it was a No 101 Sqn machine in the early 1960s. The Shahak was assigned to No 117 Sqn soon after this photograph was taken

All surviving Shahaks were painted in the standard IDF/AF camouflage scheme from 1968 onwards. Here, camouflaged aircraft 80 leads natural metal 83 on a training mission

follow me, but he didn't. I flew alone at high speed – supersonic – at about 20,000 ft, and soon saw a pair of MiG-21s flying in close formation at a similar altitude. The Egyptians flew very close, the wingman stuck to his leader – this was how they always flew in air combat. I saw them from quite a distance. I pulled up and did an aileron turn – a "stitch". I was behind them, and had started to close the distance, when IDF/AF commander Maj Gen Moti Hod ordered me to disengage. The Egyptian jets levelled their wings, lowered their noses and dived towards the Nile Delta, considerably increasing the range between us thanks to the superior acceleration of the MiG-21. I aimed at the jet pipe and launched my Atoll, but there was no chance of it hitting as the range was too great.'

Of special significance is Moti Hod's personal monitoring of the battle. In fact, this was a regular occurrence, as Hod – who also flew the Shahak, and knew its pilots individually – actually monitored air combats with a stopwatch. Each Shahak pilot had his own timeframe – one, two or three minutes – in which to achieve a kill, and when his time was up he was ordered to disengage.

On *Boxer's* final day two No 101 Sqn and four No 119 Sqn Shahaks fought Egyptian MiG-21s. No positive results were achieved, despite four of the Israeli pilots being 'top brass' in the form of Hatzor air base CO Ya'acov 'Yak' Nevo, ex-No 101 Sqn CO Amos Lapidot, No 119 Sqn CO Amos Amir and Tel Nof squadron CO Amichai 'Shumi' Shamueli. Nir recalled that it was a planned ambush;

'We flew over the swamps north-east of Ismailiya, between Tsalhiya and Mansura, at 15,000 ft at 350-400 knots. After about five minutes the Egyptians scrambled three pairs of MiG-21s. As "Shumi" and I flew south and Amos Amir and Menachem Eyal headed northwards, I saw a pair of MiG-21s pass beneath us, followed by another pair. Nobody saw them but me. We had a procedure that if a wingman saw the enemy first then he took the lead. I jettisoned my fuel tanks, expecting "Shumi" to follow, but he didn't not. I chased the trailing pair and Amos Amir and Menachem Eyal engaged the leading pair.

'My pair of MiGs flew in tight formation. They came in at high speed to fight, and it turned into a classic air combat. It took me a pretty long time, and two aileron turns ("stitching", in the vertical), to get behind them, but it wasn't very difficult. They probably saw me all the time, so when I was about 1000 m behind them they simply levelled their wings and climbed – thanks to their aircraft's superior acceleration, MiG-21 pilots often chose to disengage by levelling their wings and either diving or climbing away. My jet was armed with just a single Atoll due to the restricted number of

AA-2s available, and therefore I was quite pleased when I managed to close on the MiGs as they fled. However, I then spotted a silver Shahak converging on the MiGs at higher speed then I was. I was sure it was "Shumi" (it was actually Amos Lapidot – author).

'It was a typical situation in an air combat – two pilots chasing the same target, not seeing each other, but flying on a collision course. I could see that the Shahak was faster, and I was sure it was "Shumi". I warned him on the radio but he didn't respond, and we were now on the verge of a collision. I decided to move aside, so I broke to protect him. He was now in an ideal AAM position, although he didn't launch.

'I started to scream, "Launch, launch, launch!", but still he didn't fire. I was so angry that I positioned myself above him and launched my missile at a range of 1500 m. It exploded behind the trailing MiG, which continued to fly despite being damaged and leaking fuel. By then the MiGs had opened up the distance. I had no more AAMs, and I couldn't close the distance to cannon range because they continued to fly straight and level. I could do nothing but go home.'

Boxer resulted in a temporary scaling-down of hostilities along the Suez Canal, as well as a change in Israeli air operations that saw the IDF/AF adopt a policy of immediate response. This now meant that whenever Egyptian forces attacked, a retaliatory air strike was launched in the sector involved. The net result was that the IDF/AF operated rather like flying artillery, balancing the numerical gap between the Egyptian and Israeli artillery corps. By the second week of August, Egyptian forces had recovered from the trauma of *Boxer*. The third phase in IDF/AF involvement in the Attrition War commenced on 9 September when Israel launched a campaign, spearheaded by the IDF/AF, that was aimed at wearing down Egyptian forces in the Suez Canal and the Gulf of Suez coastal sectors.

At first the Israelis fought to achieve air supremacy through the destruction of Egyptian AAA positions, SAM sites and radar stations. This was expected to deny Egypt the option of following the static Attrition War with an offensive across the Suez Canal. It was also hoped that heavy losses would persuade the Egyptian leadership to end the static war. In other words, in the final quarter of 1969 Israel used a strategy of attrition to force Egypt to abandon the same strategy!

The campaign was launched when an Israeli armoured force, using Soviet main battle tanks and other armoured fighting vehicles captured in the Six Day War, was shipped from Sinai across the Gulf of Suez by navy landing craft. Landing near El-Hafair, the force advanced south some 50 km along the coast road, destroying anything encountered along the way. The results were significant, for about 150 Egyptian troops and a Soviet general (on advisory duty) were killed, President Nasser suffered a heart attack and the Egyptian chief of staff was dismissed. Egypt retaliated on 11 September with a massive air attack on Israeli installations in Sinai.

That day Shahaks scored seven kills for one loss – first Israeli ace Giora Rom, who became a PoW. Four of the kills were claimed in a single combat involving a No 101 Sqn pair, led by Giora Epstein, and two jets from No 117 Sqn led by Yehuda Koren, who later recalled;

'I was scrambled to intercept attacking Su-7s, but the controller gave me an altitude of 20,000 ft. Epstein was also involved, and he corrected the controller. "You are going after the MiGs at high altitude and

No 101 Sqn pilots share a joke in their ready room. They are, from left to right, Giora Epstein, Yair Sela, Shlomo Levi, Eitan Ben-Eliyahu, Yigal Shochat (seated), Oded Marom and Israel Baharav. The combined scores of Levi, Ben-Eliyahu, Epstein and Marom totalled 39.5 kills

I am going after the Sukhois at low altitude". Avsha Friedman was my wingman, and we fought six MiG-21s. Soon into the engagement two MiGs reversed, so we separated. I fought four MiGs. Avsha chased a pair and very quickly shot one of them down. I was in a left turn, and the moment one of them blew-up the rest, who were not engaged, started to escape. The aircraft that I chased levelled its wings so I launched a Shafrir 2. Avsha shouted, "Break". I broke hard and I was sure the missile missed. The aircraft on my tail overtook me, so I reversed and saw an explosion – it was my AAM.

'The MiGs fired at us from any angle. Their chances to score were slim, but they opened fire anyway. In training, when you saw a jet at such an angle you ignored it, but in this particular combat the MiGs still opened fire, and the tracers flew by. Two jets even shot at me in a head-on pass.'

The third phase of the Attrition War turned into a struggle between the IDF/AF and the Egyptian ADF. Egypt realised that any attempt to gain air superiority in the traditional way through aerial engagements was bound to fail, and in three encounters between 6 October and 27 November 1969, Shahak pilots shot down six MiG-21s. The Shahaks' monopoly was ended on 11 November 1969, however, when an F-4 Phantom II achieved a kill. From then on the Shahaks shared the glory of air-to-air victories with the much more versatile F-4, although the IDF/AF delta-fighters were credited with roughly two kills for every one achieved by a Phantom II. The IDF/AF command quickly devised tactics aimed at combining the benefits of both types, as Menachem Sharon recalled;

'We flew freely over Egypt at that time, but when the Egyptians realised we were Shahaks, and not attack aircraft, they avoided contact. However, when they identified attack aircraft, they would try to intercept them. We escorted A-4s attacking west of Suez City. The Egyptians thought there were only Skyhawks in the air, so on they came. We entered combat and the F-4s followed. I was under pressure because I was deputy CO, and most of my pilots had kills. I had not had the opportunity until then.

'We separated and I was in a one-versus-one air combat. I concentrated on that MiG and ignored the other aircraft. We turned, and I closed on him. He didn't turn very well – I think that in the right hands the Shahak turned better than the MiG. I closed on him and he made a few last desperate manoeuvres. I fired a short burst, but missed. I calmed down, and the second burst was a textbook one – the gunsight was on its fuselage, the range was 250 m and three rounds hit him. The MiG exploded and the pilot ejected.'

An Egyptian air strike on 27 November 1969 resulted in a No 117 Sqn pair, led by Shlomo Navot, being scrambled to engage the escorting MiG-21s. Yuval Ne'eman was his wingman, and he reported;

'I only saw a MiG once during the whole Attrition War. In fact, it was six years before I shot down my first MiG after becoming a Shahak pilot in 1966 . We had air superiority, so we regularly flew 30 km west of the Suez Canal. This combat started midway between Abu Sueir and Cairo – really deep over Egypt. At first the MiGs were 1500 m behind us and we got separated, which meant that we each fought a MiG. Navot downed fairly quickly and disengaged, while I fought a pilot who really knew the MiG's advantage over the Shahak. He pulled up each time I was on his tail. Every time he came down I was about 500 m behind him, shooting but not hitting. This happened several times, and I lacked the power to close the distance. I reached bingo fuel and disengaged. The MiG turned for home and didn't chase me. Only then did I realise that I hadn't jettisoned my underbelly tank!'

Even against the Shahak, a good MiG 17 pilot could hold his own. The Israelis would discover why after two Syrian MiG-17s landed in error at the small landing strip of Betzet on 12 August 1968. Shahak pilots were able to fly dissimilar air combat training (DACT) missions against them, Yitzhak Nir conducting a 'performance comparison and an air combat versus a MiG-17' in Shahak 32 on 7 November 1968. He was impressed;

'Uri Ye'ari and Ehud Henkin flew one of the MiG-17s and most Shahak pilots practiced with them. I flew against Henkin. A good MiG-17 pilot could tear a Shahak apart. I didn't realise how good this aircraft was. Henkin was incredible. He evaded me with ease, coming in right behind and closing the range with afterburner. To fight a good MiG-17 pilot at low altitude was very difficult.'

The final air combat involving Shahaks in 1969 took place over Syria when Nos 117 and 119 Sqns engaged Syrian MiG-17s and -21s. Two MiG-17s were shot down by No 119 Sqn pilots, while No 117's Uri Aven-Nir was credited with a MiG-21. Nir recalled patrolling the Golan Heights and encountering a lot of AAA;

'The Syrians scrambled two or three pairs of MiG-17s from Blai , as well as MiG-21s from other bases. They figured that we had aggressive intentions. We were vectored to engage over Blai, as was a No 117 Sqn formation. The MiG-17s were at low altitude and quite slow. At 10,000 ft, and roughly supersonic, Amos Amir (flying the jinxed Shahak 55) rolled over, saw the MiG-17s down below and dived after them. This meant a lot of "G".

The 1968/69 Term 3 conversion course, organised by No 117 Sqn, was a relatively large one, being attended by ten pilots. Seen here, standing (from left to right), are Avi Gilad, Israel Baharav, Mickey Katz, Ran Meir, Gideon Magen, Micha Gil and Shlomo Levi, with Yair Sela, Avshalom Friedman and Hertzel Bodinger crouching. Levi and Sela were assigned to No 101 Sqn, Bodinger, Friedman, Gil, Magen and Meir went to No 117 Sqn and Gilad and Katz joined No 119 Sqn. Eight of the ten later claimed kills, and three – Baharav, Levi and Gilad – became aces, while Bodinger was IDF/AF CO between 1992 and 1996

Two Syrian MiG-17s landed in error on a small strip in Israel on 12 August 1968. One of them was extensively test flown, and it is seen here wearing Israeli markings

Shahak 11 was damaged in a take-off accident in October 1969 whilst being piloted by Israel Baharav. It took IAI seven months to repair the jet

His undercarriage doors opened and the electrical system that operated the cannon failed, so he couldn't open fire. I followed him in a "split-S" and blacked-out. There I was at 7000 ft over Blai, a bit woosey, when I heard "Shahak heading east, break. There is a MiG on your tail". Am I a Shahak? Am I heading east? It must be me! I broke, but I saw nothing behind me.

'I then headed south, where I spotted two MiG-17s and two Shahaks – Uri Aven-Nir and Avshalom Friedman. I chased the trailing MiG-17. I closed the throttle, deployed my air brakes and dived after the jet, which was at about 2000 ft. I thought "If this one fights me like Ehud Henkin, it will be very bad". I was slow and my air brakes were deployed. If he had seen me, and if he had started to manoeuvre with me, it would have been very difficult, but this nice Syrian pilot didn't see me. Both pilots were fighting Aven-Nir and Friedman. They weren't aggressive, but they frustrated the Shahaks' attacks very well. Then they reversed, and this helped me cut the range to 170 m. A short burst hit the MiG-17's wing root. He immediately levelled his wings, and as I passed I saw fire coming from the wing root. The canopy blew off, the ejection seat fired and the seat separated. Then I saw a little man hanging below a red and white parachute. Because I'd opened fire at close range, many fragments hit me.

'I immediately headed home, flying low and fast to avoid AAA. There were a lot of aircraft in the air, and I was afraid someone would try to catch me if I climbed, so I only did so when I cleared the combat area. I shouted that I was hit, that I was flying to Ramat David and asked if anyone could join me. Shmul did. I flew to Ramat David, and like an idiot I buzzed and rolled. What a mistake. I landed, and it turned out that the engine was ruined. It was replaced, and a few days later I flew the aircraft to Tel Nof.'

Overall, 1969 was a very good year for Shahak pilots, with 47 kills for the loss of three aircraft. The increasing significance of the AAM was also evident with 11 kills – 23 per cent of the total – credited to the Shafrir, Shafrir 2 and the AIM-9B. The marked increase in AAM kills from three per cent in 1966-68 resulted from the introduction of more technologically-mature missiles. At the end of 1969, the leading Shahak ace was Snir with eight kills followed by Ronen (six) and Rom (five), while 24 pilots were credited with between two and four kills. A few Shahaks had also reached ace status, including aircraft 03, 59, 68, 81 and 82.

THE SOVIETS INTERVENE

By itself, Israeli air superiority could not break the military and political deadlock in the Middle East, yet it enabled a new campaign to open. The first mission of Operation *Pricha* (Blossom) was flown on 7 January 1970 when Israeli F-4s bombed three targets deep in Egypt – a commando headquarters at Inchas, a SAM training and logistics site at Dahashur and the Tel El-Kabir barracks. All targets were strictly military, but the message was aimed at the Egyptian leadership – no military installation in Egypt was immune from the F-4s. But instead of easing tensions as Israel had hoped, there was a twofold reaction.

Military training installations were transferred to Libya and there was a further escalation of the conflict, the magnitude of which was only realised in the spring of 1970. In the meantime Israeli F-4s reigned supreme over Egypt, attacking every conceivable target, with Shahaks protecting them from interception by MiG-21s.

The first Shahak kill of 1970 resulted in the emergence of Israel's fourth ace when No 101 Sqn CO Oded Marom got his fifth kill on 4 January. Four days later No 117 Sqn's Shlomo Navot achieved ace status when he downed a Syrian MiG-21. The F-4s flew five *Pricha* missions in January, and the cumulative effect of the IDF/AF offensive during the last quarter of 1969, and the deep strikes introduced in January 1970, had a devastating impact on the Egyptian ability to conduct a war of attrition. Yet, the Egyptian leadership refused to terminate hostilities without a military success. Countering the F-4s was not easy, and the Egyptian response was indeed radical. Egypt's President Nasser visited Moscow on 24-25 January, where he persuaded his hosts that the only way of easing the increasing Israeli military pressure, and avoiding another humiliating defeat, was by direct Soviet intervention.

At the time there were already 1500 Soviet advisors in Egypt, being present in every Egyptian military unit the size of a regiment and above. Several had been killed, but in early 1970 a complete Soviet air defence division, including an integral MiG-21 air brigade, began deploying to Egypt. Equipped with AAA, radar stations, command and control facilities and the latest versions of the SA-2 and SA-3 SAMs, the Soviet unit initially assumed responsibility for the defence of

Maj Gen Moti Hod, IDF/AF CO between 1966 and 1973, disembarks from Shahak 66. Hod was considered an excellent fighter pilot, and he monitored many air combats, knowing well the personal qualities of the pilots involved

Shahak 80 returns from a mission, as indicated by the missing brake 'chute housing cap just above the jet pipe nozzle. Avraham Salmon was flying this aircraft when he scored his third kill – a MiG-21 – on 8 February 1970

No 119 Sqn's regular pilots are seen outside their squadron building at Tel Nof in January 1970. They are, from left to right, Asher Snir (junior deputy CO), Yitzhak Nir, Mickey Katz, Avi Gilad, Amos Shachar, Avraham Salmon (senior deputy CO), Amos Amir (squadron commander) and Reuven Rozen. These eight pilots had a cumulative score of 53 kills at the time this photograph was taken

Alexandria, Cairo and the Aswan Dam. This freed Egyptian ADF to engage the IDF/AF in the battle for air superiority west of the Suez.

In February, Shahaks claimed five kills for two losses, while the F-4s flew six *Pricha* missions. The following month, Shahaks scored 11 kills and lost one aircraft, and the F-4s flew another six missions. Asher Snir became the first Israeli ace to take his score into double figures with his tenth kill on 27 March. Two days earlier, Giora Epstein had become the sixth Shahak ace when he claimed two kills. Israel Baharav also achieved 'acedom' on the 27th.

In April it was again the turn of No 119 Sqn to produce aces when Amos Amir and Avraham Salmon achieved their fifth kills during a major skirmish with Syrian aircraft on the 2nd. In fact, all six Shahak kills that month were credited to the unit, the most unusual coming on the night of the 24th-25th. At about 0200 hrs, Egyptian Il-28s penetrated deep into Sinai and bombed Israeli military installations in the El-Arish area.

Responding to night alerts was the responsibility of the F-4s, and although Shahak pilots continued to share this tasking, they were sceptical about their chances of being scrambled after dark. Indeed, they were so sceptical that when Amir was scrambled from Refidim to engage the Il-28s he was wearing a T-shirt, shorts and sandals! Nevertheless, he downed an Il-28. No 119 Sqn enjoyed more success three days later when the Egyptians attacked with MiG-17s and Su-7s. Yitzhak Nir recalled;

'It was very difficult to intercept them because they penetrated at low altitude, attacked close to the Suez Canal and turned back. We were scrambled from Refidim and flew really fast. I pulled up to jettison the external fuel tanks. If dropped at high speed, they rocked the wings and the AAM seeker heads could break. So until better missiles were introduced, we tried to drop the tanks at slow speed, with no excessive "G"-forces. It was quite a nuisance. If we deployed the air brakes we would have lost them, so we traded velocity for altitude. The speed decreased, the wings were levelled and we gently jettisoned the fuel tanks.

'After we dropped them I rolled over at about 7000 ft and saw four Su-7s crossing the Suez Canal. They penetrated quite deep into our territory at very low altitude. They were probably warned because they turned back towards the Canal, pushing the panic button and bombing the sand dunes. They split into two pairs, and we chased the trailing one. We descended to low level and quickly closed on them, but I flew right over the explosions from the bombs dropped by the trailing Su-7. I flew through the smoke and blast and was hit by a lot of fragments. I switched-off the afterburner and climbed. No warning light came on and the engine responded normally, but by then my wingman Dror Harish was ahead of me. I shouted, "I was hit", but it was over our territory so I wasn't worried – there was no fear of becoming a PoW. The aircraft flew, the controls responded. There was no fire and no smoke, so it was full power and back to the fight.

'Harish, meanwhile, had shot off an AAM just before we crossed the Suez Canal. I saw his missile hit. Fuel leaked out of the Su-7, but it continued to fly. Harish shouted, "I shot him down, I shot him down". I replied, "No 2, you did not shoot him down. Leave him and chase the leader. I will take the trailer". Harish calmed down, chased the leading Su-7 and shot it down with his cannon. I chased the trailing Su-7 – a damaged Shahak chasing a damaged Su-7 – and a long pursuit deep into Egypt commenced. I had two Atolls. I launched one, but it flew into the ground, so I figured the explosion of the bombs had damaged them. I decided not to launch the second AA-2.

'It was very difficult to close the range because he flew very fast – maybe 700 knots. Slowly, I closed the range, and then he noticed I was behind him. He started to turn. Maybe he was in fear, maybe he panicked – his aircraft was damaged and he saw a Shahak behind him. He could break and enter combat. It was over Egypt, and if I got low on fuel I would have left him. He just turned, helping me close the distance. I opened fire from 400 m. Three bursts and I didn't get a hit. The gunsight was in an ideal position and I was a good shot. The noise from the cannon was strange. Then I realised that one wasn't firing. The explosion of the bombs had also damaged it. I was shooting sideways. Suddenly – maybe the pilot was hit, or maybe he lost the hydraulic pressure due to the previous hits – he pitched up 90 degrees. It was obvious that no aircraft could fly like this, and that he had some sort of malfunction. I yelled into my mask, "Jump, you idiot, jump!" But he didn't. It crashed and exploded like napalm.'

The same month the unavoidable friction with the Soviets resulted in the termination of *Pricha*. Israel hoped that the USSR would now be satisfied, but once the F-4s were no longer flying deep into Egypt, the Soviets began to roll the overlapping ADF array forwards towards the Suez Canal. During May and June the IDF/AF tried targeting the Egyptian work force preparing the infrastructure for the SAM batteries, but by the end of June the Egyptians and Soviets had fought back with the destruction of two F-4s to the SAMs. Two more went down in July and a fifth in August. Israel began to lose its hard-won air superiority over the Suez Canal.

Yet to the Shahak community, it was still business as usual. Six of the eight kills in May were credited to AAMs. Snir improved his score to 11 on 12 May, and on the 14th Amir and Rozen were each credited with a MiG-21. Reuven Rozen, whose five kills were claimed in five separate engagements, explained why some fighter pilots downed more than one aircraft in a single combat;

'It was a short combat, with dramatic changes and difficult dilemmas. We were vectored into an engagement that turned out to be a classic interception. The Egyptian controller wanted to avoid combat, so he ordered the MiG-21 four-ship formation to turn 90 degrees to the left.

Yitzhak Nir shot down an Egyptian Su-7 flying Shahak 79 on 28 April 1970

The DEFA 30 mm cannon pack is displayed in front of Shahak 59 in July 1971. By this time the cannon was no longer the primary weapon for air-to-air combat following the introduction of the AIM-9D and Shafrir 2 AAMs in the late 1960s

When they finished their turn, and we flew westwards at about Mach 1.2 at 15,000 ft, we were 1500 to 2000 m behind them. Amos Amir was behind their No 4, and their No 3 was in my sights. I didn't have to do anything. The MiG-21 was in range, flying straight and level, and the missile locked on to him. I already had my finger on the switch to launch the missile when I heard Amos Amir. "No 3, pay attention. No 1 and 2 are following the trailing pair. You and No 4 chase the leading pair". I could no longer launch. I had my orders. For half a second I couldn't make up my mind. Then I pushed the switch, the missile was launched – a direct hit in the wing root. The aircraft caught fire, started to spin and the pilot ejected.

'Then I obeyed my orders. I chased the leading pair, and they were still not manoeuvring. I opened fire at 350 m, but my aim was poor. When you shot down an aircraft it was like having an orgasm. You then had to return to the hunt, but I felt elated. I thought to myself, "I downed a MiG", not "I have to down this one as well", so my aim wasn't good.

'At that stage, flying supersonic at 15,000 ft, the MiG rolled over. My gunsight was pointing below its cockpit, and I'm sure that if I had opened fire at that moment I would have hit him. But I was sure he would drop his nose. If I hadn't reacted quickly, I would have lost my advantage. Should have I preserved it? If I had shot him down, then my advantage would have been meaningless. That is exactly what I should have done, but I decided to preserve my advantage. I didn't open fire and rolled over. He dropped his nose and I could see the green Nile Delta straight ahead. I closed on the MiG, down to about 100 m. I couldn't miss, but then I correctly decided not to open fire. It was too close.

'Suddenly, I felt the stick was heavy and remembered that the limit for a supersonic dive was 30 degrees. Obviously it was not the time to remember such a thing – I should have done so before starting the dive. The MiG-21 had elevators and he started to recover, while I was diving towards the ground with my wingman following. I throttled back and deployed the air brakes. I decelerated to subsonic speed and still had to pull 10G to recover. I blacked out, and I couldn't even see if my recovery was successful.

'I had gone from shooting down one aircraft and nearly destroying a second, to blacking out, without knowing if I was going to be killed or not, in just a matter of minutes! Moreover, that MiG was somewhere up there, and even if I could recover, all he had to do was open fire at me. I was at a tactical disadvantage even if I survived the dive. When I realised my nose was above the horizon, I unloaded. My eyesight recovered and I looked for the MiG. Instead of chasing us he had disengaged.'

The next day two additional aces emerged – Yehuda Koren and Kobi Richter. That brought the total number of Shahak aces to 11. Yehuda Koren recalled;

'We patrolled and the controller joined us up with a No 119 Sqn pair, led by Salmon. They led and we trailed them. When we turned south

Developed in Israel by IAI, the Shafrir 2 proved to be a crucial weapon for the IDF/AF. Indeed, its service introduction resulted in a dramatic shift in the number of kills scored with cannon in favour of the modern guided weapon. Initially equipping the Shahaks of No 117 Sqn (No 101 Sqn preferred the American AIM-9D), the Shafrir 2 was also used by the two new Nesher squadrons formed in 1972-73. The only setback in the Shafrir 2's operational career came in 1972 when No 117 Sqn's Shahaks failed in their attempts to shoot down Syrian Su-7s with the missile, while No 101 Sqn enjoyed successes with the AIM-9D. It then became apparent that the Shafrir 2's seeker head had been optimised for the MiG-21's heat signature. The problem was quickly rectified, and many Sukhois fell to Shafrir 2s during the Yom Kippur War. One of those to subsequently enjoy success with the missile during this conflict was Menachem Sharon, who shot down a MiG-17 with a Shafrir 2 on 8 October 1973, flying Nesher 28. He remembers, 'The AIM-9D had a cooled seeker head, so, theoretically, it enjoyed a better launch envelope. It was also sleeker in appearance and produced less drag than the bulky Shafrir 2. However, the Shafrir 2 was simply a killer. The AIM-9D guided smoothly while the Shafrir 2 flew like crazy, with significant control inputs in flight. My squadron achieved 23 kills from 45 Shafrir 2 launches – an enormous achievement at the time'

I became the leader, and I soon spotted a MiG-21 which, in my opinion, had not seen me. We well into Egyptian territory, in the area of Inchas and Bilbeis. I launched my AAM from quite a distance – maybe 2000 m. Typically, when you launched a missile at a shorter range, its rocket was still burning when it hit the aircraft. In this case the missile's rocket flamed-out, and I thought I had missed. But then came the explosion.'

Eight kills were also credited to the Shahak community in June, while on 10 July Yiftach Spector also achieved ace status. Undisciplined behaviour surfaced again in the latter combat, but the IDF/AF took the view that it was better to bridle lively horses than having lazy ones in need of the whip. Israel Baharav recalled;

'I was a leader, but when a team was organised to shoot down MiGs I flew as wingman. We came as a team to shoot down MiGs, joining attack aircraft on a bombing mission. We came in with them during their bombing runs. By then the Egyptians were thoroughly familiar with our deception tactics, and they only tried to intercept our attack aircraft. We therefore hoped to surprise them on this occasion.

'When we spotted the MiGs on radar we quickly sent the attackers home. Flying west, we rapidly closed the distance between us, but it turned out that we were actually chasing their jettisoned external fuel tanks! They had detected our ruse and disengaged. The Egyptians had also prepared an ambush for us in the form of a four-ship formation at low altitude. We all saw a pair of MiG-21s pulling up after our leading pair, and I knew they would not be alone – another pair, maybe more, was surely behind us. Sure enough, I spotted two more jets heading in our direction. I reported, "No 3, there's another pair coming in on our tail. I'm turning right into them". Sharon replied, "Negative. Stay with me – the target is straight ahead". Spector knew that I had the reputation of being an undisciplined pilot, so he said, "No 4, stay with No 3". I had no choice, so I said, "No 3, I'll go left and you go right and up. Pull-up and join me".

'The MiGs were so fast that they pulled-up and I couldn't catch them. They then tried to dive and disengage. I tried to follow, but couldn't get close to them. Then they pulled up and dived once again. They did this three times. I couldn't catch them – not during the pull-up and not during the dive. The third time they entered a steep 60-degree dive – a crazy supersonic dive. They flew very close to each other, and I launched a missile at the leading MiG. As the missile exploded he rolled over into a "split-S" at 60 degrees, 10,000 ft and Mach 1.4. His wingman rolled after him and I started to roll, but realised that I wouldn't be able to recover. I decided it was too dangerous, so I rolled back.

'I could see the trailing MiG also roll back, but I could no longer see the leading MiG. I recovered from that manoeuvre at 2000 ft with my G-meter at the maximum 10 G. My generator and alternator ceased to

Israel Baharav achieved one of his five double MiG-21 kills flying Shahak 59 on 10 July 1970 – the 10th and 11th kills scored in this well-known fighter. Seen here just prior to being painted in camouflage colours, the aircraft displays only ten victory symbols. This discrepancy was duly corrected during the painting process. Displayed at a base open day just six days after Baharav's 10 July successes, the aircraft has been loaded up in CAP configuration, with two supersonic 500-litre underwing fuel tanks and a single R.530 on the centreline pylon. By this time, however, the French SARH AAM was hardly ever used, as the far superior F-4/AIM-7 combination was by now a tried and tested part of the frontline IDF/AF

function momentarily due to the high G-load recovery, and I had to revive the systems. I then saw the trailing MiG recover below me and the leading MiG crash.

'I then started a long chase after the trailing MiG. There were very low clouds over the Nile Delta, and he flew towards his base at Mansura. I tried to stop him getting into the clouds, but I wasn't close enough and he disappeared. The grounds were very low, barely 200-300 ft above the ground. I opened fire into the cloud and then descended below it. Sharon descended below the cloud too, and there was my MiG in flames, its pilot ejecting close to his base at Mansura. I had fired into the cloud – an extraordinary kill!'

The IDF/AF used the team concept quite often, and its best-known exploitation came in combat with the Soviets on 30 July. By the end of the month Israel had already lost four F-4s, and the expansion of the Soviet-backed Egyptian ADF coverage continued. Sensing success, the Soviet pilots probably wanted to imitate the achievements of their ground-based comrades. On 25 July Soviet-flown MiG-21s intercepted Israeli A-4s, one of which was hit by an AA-2, although the damaged jet made it safely back to base. With the Soviets winning the struggle for air superiority over the Suez Canal, Israel decided to teach them a lesson.

An ambush was planned – for 30 July – and a team of experts assembled. Each Shahak unit contributed a four-ship formation. Those from Nos 117 and 119 Sqns, together with four F-4s, were to be in the air, while a No 101 Sqn formation was held on immediate alert at Refidim. The No 119 Sqn Shahaks were to imitate jets on a reconnaissance mission by flying at high altitude over an area defended by Soviet MiG-21s. If the latter scrambled to intercept what they thought were two Shahaks flying straight and level at 35,000 ft, they would instead be faced with four fully-armed jets. Lurking at low altitude beyond the reach of Egyptian and Soviet radar systems would be the No 117 Sqn Shahaks and the F-4s.

The Soviets fell into the trap and scrambled several four-ship formations into. A multi-bogey engagement soon developed, at the heart of which were the four No 119 Sqn Shahaks flown by Amos Amir, Asher Snir, Avraham Salmon and Avi Gilad, who between them shared a total of 26 kills.

As the first Soviet MiG formation approached, the hunters became the hunted. Salmon was the first to shoot down a MiG, quickly followed by Snir. Immediately afterwards Snir was hit by an AA-2, but he managed to disengage and nurse his damaged jet back to Refidim.

Meanwhile, two additional four-ship formations of Soviet-flown

High-altitude Shahak reconnaissance flights were introduced in July 1970 to counter the threat posed by improved Egyptian SAM defences. No 119 Sqn Shahaks 19, 41, 68, 78 and 85 also participated in the reconnaissance effort, in addition to dedicated aircraft Nos 98 and 99

Avraham Salmon, flying Shahak 78, shot down a Soviet MiG-21 and shared another with Yiftach Spector on 30 July 1970

No 101 Sqn pilots pose for the camera at Hatzor on 24 June 1971. They are, in the front row from left to right, Yoram Geva, Michael Haber, Dan Sever, Giora Epstein (senior deputy CO), Yiftach Spector (squadron commander), Michael Zuk (junior deputy CO) and Amos Shachar, and in the back row, left to right, Ilan Auerbuch, Gidon Dror, Reuven Rozen, Eliezer Ye'ari, Eitan Karmi and Moshe Hertz. This group of 13 pilots includes five reservists (Dror, Haber, Karmi, Rozen and Sever), all of whom were 'MiG killers' with a cumulative score of 80.5 victories

No 119 Sqn lines its Shahaks up in a farewell formation prior to flying a final fly-past with the aircraft on 8 October 1970. Shahaks 03, 19, 41, 58, 78, 85, 89, 98 and 99 were transferred to No 101 Sqn, while 32, 66, 68, 79, 80 and 83 went to No 117 Sqn

MiG-21s approached the area, as did the F-4s and the No 117 Sqn Shahaks, with Uri Aven-Nir leading Ithamar Neuner, Yehuda Koren and Kobi Richter – four pilots with a cumulative score of 20 kills. Just after the No 117 Sqn formation was vectored to engage, the engine oil warning light came on in Neuner's cockpit. Aven-Nir aborted the mission and escorted Neuner back to Refidim, from where a No 101 Sqn pair led by Yiftach Spector was scrambled to replace them.

Five MiG-21s were downed during this encounter, for in addition to the initial pair claimed by No 119 Sqn, a further two jets were destroyed by the F-4s. The fifth kill was shared by Salmon and Spector. This amazing victory helped balance the success of the Soviet-backed Egyptian ADF. More significantly, it meant that both sides could now give in gracefully to US diplomatic pressure and end a regional conflict which had the potential to develop into a clash between the USA and the USSR.

ENTER THE NESHER

In 1971 Shahak pilots had a kill-free year – this had no happened since 1966. The community had shrunk the previous October when No 119 Sqn ceased operating the Shahak due to fleet attrition. However, by 1971 the delta-fighter community was growing again with the arrival of the IAI Nesher (Eagle), which was in effect a locally-produced Mirage 5.

Initial Nesher deliveries augmented the strength of Nos 101 and 117 Sqns, but the side-by-side operation of the two types resulted in unfair comparisons being made. The Nesher was heavier, with a higher fuel fraction, so no mixed formations were flown for it was thought that Shahak pilots would have to disengage from combat before the Neshers. The Nesher was also a better fighter-bomber, and in a mixed formation on an air-to-ground mission, the Shahak's presence would be a handicap.

Surprisingly, Nesher pilots were unable to exploit all their advantages against the Shahaks in dissimilar air combat training, where agility and manoeuvrability counted. Such training sessions ended when one of the participants reached bingo fuel. Frustrated pilots immediately preferred the Shahak, but in combat the differences between the Nesher and the Shahak did not seem that significant, although the Nesher's better

This view of the Nesher's cockpit reveals the absence of a radar scope in the IAI-engineered fighter-bomber – the Cyrano's scope dominated the Shahak's cockpit. The panel to the right of the gunsight was reserved for the radar warning receiver, while a stores management system was added just above the pilot's right knee

These pilots helped form Nesher-equipped No 144 Sqn. They are, from left to right, Giora Goren (senior deputy CO), Uri Aven-Nir (CO), Mikey Avrahami, Yermi Keidar (junior deputy CO), Ya'acov Piada and Eli Menachem

Below and right
Yoram Geva scored the Nesher's first kill in aircraft 16 on 8 January 1973. Although the jet is seen here equipped with Shafrir 2s, Geva claimed his victory with an AIM-9D

combat endurance was of great importance. IAI test pilot Assaf Ben-Nun recalled;

'We called the Shahak a sports aircraft. Obviously the Shahak manoeuvred better than the Nesher. The extra ton of fuel carried by the Nesher couldn't be dismissed since the Shahak carried 2.5 tons of fuel and the Nesher 3.5 tons – a most significant difference. The Shahak was far more restricted by its limited fuel, and in most of my Yom Kippur War air combats I would not have shot down enemy aircraft if I'd been flying a Shahak. The Shahak was better to fly, it was more manoeuvrable and it flew smoother, but pilots who had enjoyed years of success with the jet also inflated its reputation. Although the Shahak manoeuvred better, it didn't shoot down as many aircraft as the Nesher during the Yom Kippur War.

'If the Nesher had had the Shahak's manoeuvrability, it might have performed even better. But from an operational point of view, it turned out that the additional fuel was far more important than the minimal loss in handling. If you flew a Shahak with two external 500-litre fuel tanks, then you had the same fuel as a smooth Nesher with internal fuel only. In my opinion, a clean Nesher was superior to a Shahak with two external fuel tanks.'

By 1973 the delta-fighter community had actually doubled in size, with the forming of No 144 Sqn at Etszion air base in 1972, followed by No 113 Sqn at Hatzor. These two units were homogeneous Nesher operators, while No 117 Sqn returned to being an all-Shahak unit, leaving No 101 Sqn as the only heterogeneous one. The delta-fighter community's expansion resulted in the induction of fresh blood, new young pilots arriving in the frontline just only eight to twelve months after graduation from fighter school. Zvika Vered, who started flying the Shahak in 1971 – only eight months after earning his wings – recalled;

'There were no video cameras in the jets – only gunsight cameras, which captured up to five seconds of an air combat manoeuvring training (ACM) sortie. So, during debriefing, a pilot could replay only a few seconds from his gunsight film. There were only a few two-seat aircraft, so it was mostly self-learning while flying the single-seaters. Ran Meir was a fantastic pilot and a phenomenon in ACM training, but it was very difficult for him to share his knowledge with us. Had we had today's debriefing technology back then, it would have been much more simple.'

Activity was restricted to 'combat days', a term that defined concentrated flying on a single day, with the delta-fighters either defending a recce mission or protecting attack aircraft. In five such days between September 1972 and September 1973 the delta-fighters were credited with 14 kills, only one of which was achieved with the cannon. No new aces emerged, but seven pilots scored their first kills. A typical engagement, resulting in two maiden kills for the pilots involved, came on 21 November 1972 when No 117 Sqn senior deputy CO, Yuval Ne'eman, led Zvika Vered to intercept Syrian MiG-21s, as the latter recalled;

'It was a simple engagement. The F-4s were leading and we trailed behind. They were searching for targets, looking inside the cockpit, but saw nothing, yet we visually identified the MiGs! We were flying at 20,000 ft above the AAA ceiling, and Ne'eman saw the MiGs down below chasing F-4s which had just completed an attack mission. We dived right after them and I launched an AAM. The other MiG saw my missile and broke, so Ne'eman had to turn with him. My AAM hit the MiG. It exploded and I didn't see an ejection. When Ne'eman finally shot down his MiG he was quite excited, so he asked me, "Two, where are you?" I had followed him all that time.

'That same afternoon I called my father on the 'phone and he said to me, "greetings". I was surprised. The engagement was reported on the radio, but how did he know that it was me who had shot down a MiG? I asked him, and he replied, "What do you mean? It's your birthday today!"'

No 117 Sqn senior deputy CO Yuval Ne'eman is greeted by jubilant groundcrewmen after shooting down a MiG-21 on 21 November 1972. It was the squadron's custom to carry successful pilots shoulder-high in triumph from the cockpit to the squadron building

Zvika Vered was also victorious on 21 November 1972, downing a second MiG-21 in Shahak 79. And like Yuval Ne'eman, he too was carried triumphantly from his jet to the crewroom at Ramat David

CHAPTER FIVE

YOM KIPPUR WAR

In March 1971 Yermi Keidar became the second pilot to be seriously injured in a landing accident in the jinxed Shahak 55. He was unconscious for seven days, suffering from head and internal injuries, a mangled hand and fingers and a smashed leg. Nine months later he left hospital with one leg two inches shorter than the other, restricted ankle movement and a desire to fly jet fighters again. But his injuries was so severe that nobody paid any attention to his request – nobody, that is, except IDF/AF CO Maj Gen Beni Peled and No 101 Sqn CO Avi Lanir. The medical experts concluded that if Keidar had to eject again his leg was doomed, and that he would never be fit to fly jet fighters.

Yet, on 5 May 1972, he returned to fly the Shahak following a brief check-out with Lanir in a two-seater. The following year Keidar was certainly fit enough to become involved in the first aerial engagement of the conflict that came to be known as the Yom Kippur War.

Yom Kippur is the Jewish Day of Atonement, a day when everything stops in Israel – no traffic, no radio, no television and certainly no flying. But on the morning of Yom Kippur – 6 October 1973 – at Etszion, No 144 Sqn CO Menachem Sharon ordered his senior deputy, Yermi Keidar, to organise a four-ship formation to fly a CAP for a reconnaissance mission along the Suez Canal. The objective was to verify intelligence reports that war was imminent. The squadron was already on alert with EP and reserve pilots present. Keidar selected two of the latter to fly as his Nos 2 and 3, with a regular pilot as his No 4. His time over target was 1400 hrs, and he recalled;

'We flew at low altitude to a certain point, from where we had to pull up to fly the CAP. En route, I searched the sky, but couldn't see the recce aircraft – no vapours, nothing. It was strange. Two minutes before the planned pull-up time, the controller broke radio silence and called me, "Madrid. Engage 270". At first I panicked. I thought I was behind schedule, but immediately realised that I wasn't ordered to climb but to engage!

'The controller said the enemy aircraft were above Om Hashiba at such an altitude that I had to climb to 10,000 ft, but I saw nothing. The controller then said, "They are at low altitude", so we dived, but still saw nothing. Again the controller said, "They're at 8000 ft", so we climbed again. It turned out that the controller didn't have a real-time aerial picture, so he was using intelligence information. We repeatedly dived and climbed. Suddenly, as I was climbing at about 7000-8000 ft, I saw them – four Su-7s at low altitude, maybe 300 ft above ground

Following reports as early as 8 October that Libyan Mirages were operating from Egypt, the Israeli delta-fighters were painted with black outlined yellow identification triangles. The first engagement between Israeli and Libyan Mirages came on the 18th

level. We jettisoned our external fuel tanks and dived right behind them, Assaf on my left, Shmul and Lavi on my right. I gave Assaf enough space to chase the trailing Su-7, and got organised behind the No 3 Su-7 flying parallel with the Su-7 being chased by Assaf. I launched a Shafrir 2 and it homed perfectly, passing very close to the Su-7's nozzle. But it didn't explode – probably a proximity fuse failure. At that moment I saw a huge explosion on my left, and the Su-7 flying in parallel with me simply vanished. Assaf had shot down his Sukhoi.'

Flying Nesher 15, IAI test pilot Assaf Ben-Nun scored the IDF/AF's first kill of the Yom Kippur War on the afternoon of 6 October 1973

Assaf Ben-Nun was duly credited with the first kill of the Yom Kippur War. A reserve pilot since 1960, he was one of the few flying fighters. In the 1956 Sinai campaign he had flown the P-51D as a regular pilot, and then the Mystere during the Six Day War. In both conflicts he was shot down, yet was credited with his first kill during the Six Day War. Ben-Nun was an agricultural pilot from 1960 to 1968, when he joined IAI as a test pilot. If anyone deserved the honour of downing an aircraft in an IAI product, it was certainly the Kfir project chief test pilot. He recalled;

'We saw four Su-7s flying at low altitude. Yermi was just a little ahead of me and pretty much on my right. He was behind an Su-7. So was I, in good AAM range. I heard the beep indicating target acquisition, so I launched the missile, but nothing happened. The Su-7s flew at low altitude and visibility wasn't good – there was a haze. I looked into my cockpit and switched the selector to the other missile. When I looked out again I couldn't see the Su-7, but still heard that beep. I saw Yermi on my right and was sure the AAM wasn't locked-on to his aircraft. I couldn't see the Su-7, but decided to launch without seeing the target. As I followed the missile, I saw the Su-7 again. The missile hit the Sukhoi and it exploded – the first kill in the Yom Kippur War.'

Immediately afterwards, Keidar shot down his Su-7. He saw the pilot ejecting just as he avoided another jet being chased by Shmul. Also an IAI test pilot, Shmul was to become the 13th Israeli ace, and the first of the Yom Kippur War. But now the controller was yelling for help as the ground control station came under attack by radar-homing AS-5 ASMs launched by Egyptian Tu-16s. The controller urged Keidar to fly a CAP above the station, but the latter was still not fully satisfied as the Nesher pilots had only shot down three Su-7s, leaving the Egyptian formation leader still target-bound. He ordered Shmul to lead Ben-Nun on a CAP over Refidim, while he set off in lone pursuit of the leading Su-7. Ben-Nun thought he had figured out the Su-7s' route, so he accelerated to supersonic speed at very low altitude, half a minute behind the Sukhoi.

'I flew low over a road leading to a junction where there was a large IDF Armoured Corps camp. The sun was behind me, and I was looking for the Su-7's shadow on the ground. In the distance, I saw the barracks, and then I saw him. He climbed a little during the turn – a regular practice to avoid flying into the ground during a high-rate, high-speed turn at low altitude. I cut across his path just as he levelled his wings. I was 1000-1500 m behind him. I launched my second missile and it flew straight into the jet pipe. There was a huge explosion and the aircraft vanished – there was no ejection. This guy was dedicated to his mission. Maybe they flew in radio silence, so he may not have been aware of Assaf's kill. However, the pilot ejected from the first Su-7 that I downed, and Shmul got a Sukhoi that had actually engaged us, so they probably did break radio silence. The lead pilot still pressed-on with his mission.'

Having accounted for all four Su-7s, the Neshers flew a CAP over Refidim until they were relieved by another formation. By then their fuel state was critically low, and Etszion was too far away. Refidim's runway had been cratered by an Egyptian attack, but Yosef Lavi still managed to land at the base, leaving the three remaining Neshers to fly on to El-Arish. Assaf Ben-Nun recalled that they landed at the latter base out of the blue;

'The base commander was asleep, and he didn't know that there was a war on! There were tankers to refuel and generators to start our engines, but no delta groundcrews. As a test pilot, I knew the Nesher pretty well. I knew that several underbelly doors had to be opened to refuel it. There was a cock that we called the five taps handle. Once it was pulled it was possible to refuel the aircraft single-point. We pulled it but it was stuck – it didn't move. I tried to 'phone Etszion to ask for advice, but the military telephone network had simply collapsed. It was impossible to contact anybody. I remembered the home 'phone number of our IAI line chief, Uri Bat – a civilian. I asked him, "Uri, how do you refuel the aircraft? We can't pull the five taps handle". He explained that first you had to release the pressure in the system, and only then pull the handle. We did, and refuelled the aircraft. Darkness had fallen by then, and we had no braking 'chutes. Nevertheless, we flew over a completely blacked-out nation and landed at Etszion without braking 'chutes.'

By the end of the day the delta-fighters had been credited with eight kills, but the simultaneous Egyptian and Syrian attack had been successful. Egyptian forces had gained a firm foothold along the eastern bank of the Suez Canal, while the Syrians had occupied the southern part of the Golan Heights, as well as the strategically important Mount Hermon. Immediate IDF mobilisation slowly changed the balance at the two front-lines. Initial

Zvika Vered claimed a Syrian MiG-21 in Shahak 07 on 7 October 1973, despite having entered combat with an alternator malfunction that robbed him of his AAMs and afterburner

Israeli counter-attacks met with success in the north but failed in the south. As a result, the Egyptian front was relatively static between 8 and 14 October, while in the north the Syrian forces were pushed back until Damascus came within range of Israeli artillery.

It was on 7 October that No 117 Sqn's Zvika Vered demonstrated the delta fighter pilots' devotion to duty. He described what happened;

'Elisha Peri and I were scrambled to assist Avsha Friedman and Dani Shlaider, who were fighting eight MiG-21s. When we took-off I noticed an alternator malfunction. Half my systems didn't function, including the AAMs and the afterburner. But we pressed-on. There was an emergency afterburner ignition system which bypassed the primary one – you poured fuel into the afterburner and it ignited. The resulting "big bang" could damage the engine, but it was an emergency. We came in very fast. I selected a target and knew I had only one chance to get him with my cannon. I opened fire from 1000 m and didn't stop until I had shot him down. It was a long burst that nearly exhausted my ammunition – I couldn't operate my AAMs. I had hardly any ammunition left, so I said to Elisha, "Let's get the hell out of here". That's exactly what we did. We came in, I got a MiG and we disengaged.'

The Shahaks flew daytime air-to-air sorties and the Neshers also flew some air-to-ground missions. Geographically, No 117 Sqn operated over the northern front, and all its kills were Syrian aircraft, while No 144 Sqn flew mostly over the south, so its successes were against the Egyptians. Hatzor-based Nos 101 and 113 Sqns operated over both fronts, and also shared the Refidim alert duty.

The two primary missions were alerts and CAPs, with three sorties a day not being uncommon for pilots. Many hours were also spent in the cockpit on alert. Most scrambles did not result in an engagement, and often simply meant that a pilot who had spent an hour or two in the cockpit on alert then had to fly a CAP of up to 90 minutes' duration. Once he returned, the procedure was repeated. The burden was high and the mental stress considerable, but the delta-fighter pilots felt their personal risk was not as great as the sacrifice being made by their brethren flying attack aircraft, who flew into danger on every single mission, day or night.

There was no shortage of enthusiasm for shooting down enemy aircraft, and quite a number of delta-fighters were lost as pilots pursued their mission against all odds, flying low over dense AAA. Commanders, who had difficulty imposing discipline, stressed that preservation of the force was more important than taking risks to down a MiG-17. Yet they were anxious not to suppress pilots' eagerness and initiative. Another problem was that of jettisoning external fuel tanks. The procedure was to do so once a formation had been vectored to engage, but it soon became apparent that this did not usually result in combat. The waste was astonishing, with each squadron jettisoning some 50 tanks a day! Moreover, once tanks had been

No 113 Sqn's Nesher 23 is prepared for a mission during the Yom Kippur War, the jet carrying two supersonic 500-litre tanks under the wings and a single 880-litre tank under the fuselage. The wastage rate of fuel tanks was alarmingly high at the start of the war, and groundcrews often did not have time to remove the red protective paint when they were removed from emergency storage facilities. Pilots were soon ordered to jettison their wing tanks *only* when visual contact with the enemy had been made. The under-fuselage tank was shed only when absolutely necessary

No 101 Sqn groundcrews work on Shahak 51 during the war. During the Yom Kippur War, pilots flying this jet claimed a MiG-21 and an Su-7 destroyed, as well as a MiG-21 and an Su-7 shared destroyed. The latter was a Syrian Sukhoi shared with No 117 Sqn Shahak 83 on 10 October 1973

CHAPTER FIVE

Dror Harish was credited with two Syrian MiG-17s destroyed in Shahak 52 on 9 October 1973, these being added to his four previous victories to make him an ace. This aircraft had already been used to score six kills prior to Harish's successes

This fireball, seen through the gunsight of Avraham Salmon's Nesher, saved six Egyptian MiG-17s on 18 October 1973. Seconds later, Salmon's windscreen was covered with debris, thus preventing him from shooting down any further MiGs. The explosion was caused when a seventh MiG-17 was downed by Gidon Dror, who hit it with a Shafrir 2. The vision from Dror's Nesher was also badly obscured, forcing him to break off the chase as well

No 113 Sqn EP pilot Ilan Gonen and reserve pilot Avi Gilad were both credited with single MiG-21 kills on 23 October 1973

jettisoned the delta-fighters were unable to return to fly a CAP. The procedure was therefore changed so that external tanks were jettisoned only after pilots visually acquired their targets, while underbelly tanks were not usually shed, as the performance penalty incurred with this store was not significant.

The first three days of the war saw the delta-fighters committed to both fronts. On the first day, seven of the eight kills were on the Egyptian front, falling to two out of eleven on the second day, when the IDF/AF launched a disastrous offensive against the Syrian ADF. Seventeen of the twenty kills on 8 October came on the Egyptian front, following a failed Israeli counter-offensive. The next day all delta-fighter kills were on the Syrian front. That was also when No 101 Sqn reserve pilot Dror Harish became an ace. Four days later Ithamar Neuner also 'made ace', as did Reuven Rozen on the 13th. The latter date also saw Ra'anan Yosef credited with his first kill;

'I was flying a CAP with Ilan Gonen when we saw explosions. We weren't actually vectored to engage. I visually locked-on to a MiG-17. I launched a Shafrir 2, and five to ten seconds later Gonen launched at the same MiG. I saw mine hit. There was an explosion and then Gonen's AAM hit the fireball. I saw another MiG-17, but I was flying too fast, so I climbed. The weather was pretty cloudy, and when I dived again I saw nobody – not the MiG-17, not Gonen. Alone, I flew east, searching for the other MiG, but saw nothing. I was already deep into enemy territory, so I turned back and rejoined Ilan. I was elated. It was my first kill, and then I heard Avi Lanir on the radio. He was leading a pair to replace us on the CAP. It was the last time I heard his voice.'

Four delta fighters had already been lost over the Syrian front, at least two of which fell to AAA and SAMs while chasing enemy fighters. The fifth loss was No 101 Sqn CO Avi Lanir, who was shot down by an SA-3 during a pursuit. Following Zvi Vered's loss on 9 October, Ramat David

No 117 Sqn's Shahak 50

base CO Ya'acov Agassi ordered all No 117 Sqn pilots to avoid known SAM areas while pursuing enemy aircraft. Nevertheless, Amichai Roke'ach went in similar circumstances on the 12th.

Immediately after Lanir's loss, IDF/AF CO Maj Gen Beni Peled issued a strict order banning delta-fighter pilots from crossing the forward line of troops (FLOT) during pursuits on the Syrian front. If a pilot managed to shoot down a Syrian aircraft west of the FLOT then fine, but a long pursuit east was not considered worth the risk of exposure to AAA and SAM batteries. But Reuven Rozen was in the cockpit on alert when this order was issued, and was therefore unaware of the new directive. He said;

'I saw two Su-20s, but the controller said, "They're ours". This confusion cost me a quick kill, for I was right behind them. I closed and saw the aircrafts' numbers in Arabic, but by then they were already escaping at low altitude and high speed – 680 knots. We crossed the FLOT. They flew in line abreast. I chased the right-hand Su-20 and my wingman was behind me. I launched an AAM. There was an explosion, but the jet kept flying.

'There was a lot of AAA fire and SAMs, which I ignored, but I saw AAA hit the Su-20's wingtip. I launched my second AAM and it was just like the first – an explosion from which he emerged and continued to fly. The controller reported to his superiors that there was a pursuit, and he was ordered to bring me back. He screamed, "Return immediately", but I didn't answer. It was difficult enough to fly at such high speed and at such low altitude and handle the radio as well.

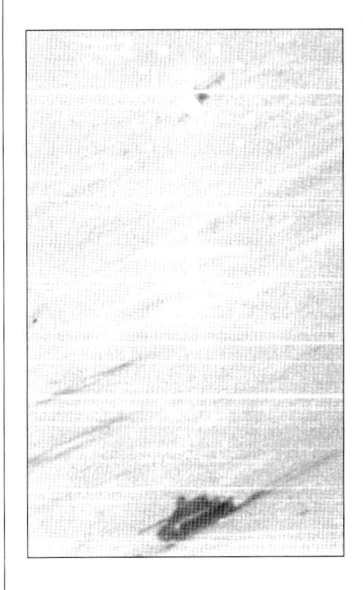

The hazard of fighting enemy aircraft over the forward line of troops (FLOT) is clearly illustrated by this Nesher gunsight image. Flying low over hostile territory, focusing on a small target above the battlefield, exposed pilots to numerous threats – small arms fire, the deadly ZSU-23 quad AAA, shoulder-launched SA-7s, mobile SA-6s and SA-2 and SA-3 systems

Sitting alert in the cockpit was a task hated by most pilots, and the fortunate ones were those who were scrambled immediately. Most had to sit there for hours, and when they were finally scrambled, endured a further 90 minutes on CAP. Elisha Peri recalled, 'I flew 44 sorties during the war. We spent a lot of time in the cockpit – daytime alert, two or three sorties per day, eight-nine hours in the cockpit per day'

'By then we were far behind the FLOT, and there was no AAA fire or SAMs. I managed to close, but couldn't open fire. I had to be slightly lower than he was in order to use my cannon, but we were flying so low that it was impossible. Suddenly, we overflew a depression in the terrain, and this was my opportunity. I opened fire and he crashed. If I'd had AAMs I would have chased the second Su-20, but I was deep into Syria with no missiles left. I then had a brilliant idea of which I'm proud to this day. I had no fuel problem because I had jettisoned the tanks *after* I had launched the first AAM, so why return via the hell of Syrian SAMs and AAA fire? I rejoined my wingman and we flew home via Mafraq, Amman and Jerusalem, circumnavigating the Golan Heights frontline.

'When I landed, the squadron CO told me, "You are grounded until the end of the war by order of the IDF/AF CO. He ordered no pursuit. You violated his order and you are grounded". I replied, "I didn't hear. I was on alert in the aircraft", but I was still grounded. That afternoon no recce pilots were available, so I flew an escort mission with No 101 Sqn. That night Hatzor base CO Amos Lapidot met Maj Gen Beni Peled, and he managed to explain my situation. Next day I was flying again.'

Israel's second highest-scoring ace Shlomo Levi had a particularly successful day on 12 October. He was leading Lapidot on a CAP at 18,000 ft when they were warned by the ground controller of enemy aircraft. Levi later reported;

'The ground controller said, "Elite engage, 090 full power". We jettisoned our external under-wing fuel tanks, switched on afterburner, accelerated and tested our cannon. We over-flew the Golan Heights at low altitude to avoid the SAMs, and Amos was the first to spot them. They came from the east in a shallow dive, flying north. We decelerated, jettisoned our underbelly tanks and turned north. But as they were in a dive, and we had decelerated, the distance between us opened up. They disappeared in the smoke of war. We flew north, low and fast – about 600 knots at 300 ft AGL – trying to locate them through the haze and smoke. Then I noticed a pair of Shahaks overtaking me. Neither the controller or the Shahak pilots said a word. I noticed that they had white-painted Shafrir 2 AAMs, so I figured that they were from No 117 Sqn. They launched a missile, but it hit the ground and they also disappeared from my sight into the haze.

'We were already flying over the northern sector of the Golan Heights when suddenly I saw an aircraft. From behind it could have been an Su-7. I could also have been a Shahak, and I didn't know whether to open fire or not. The range was about 1500 m, causing my AAMs to beep. The

No 113 Sqn junior deputy CO Shlomo Levi became an ace in Nesher 14 on 16 October 1973. With ten kills, Levi was the second-ranked Yom Kippur War ace, his score surpassed only by Giora Epstein with 12

Shlomo Levi shot down three Syrian Sukhois in one engagement flying this aircraft, Nesher 21, on 12 October 1973. The first two were downed by Shafrir 2 missiles – six of Levi's total of ten kills were achieved with the Israeli missile. He later commented, 'I know absolutely nothing about success rates and launch-to-kill ratios. I only know that I launched six Shafrir 2 missiles and got six kills!'

aircraft turned north-west, and I didn't know what to do. Finally, I decided to climb a little and saw that it was a Sukhoi. I descended, launched an AAM, saw the explosion and noticed that the aircraft continued to fly, turning right towards Mount Hermon. I didn't follow, as I now realised that there were actually two Sukhois. I switched to the second jet, launching my remaining AAM and half-pushing the cannon trigger so that the gun camera operated. The missile hit the Sukhoi, which started to bank – the pilot ejected.

'Suddenly, I saw another Su-7. Having no more AAMs, I closed the range to 400 m and opened fire. All sorts of bits and pieces flew off the aircraft and then it actually seemed to stop in the air. I overtook the jet and it flick-rolled into the ground. The next thing I noticed was that I was over Damascus, so I immediately turned left and returned home.'

By the 14th the Syrian capital was within Israeli artillery range. The same day Egypt launched an offensive which resulted in the destruction of 200 of its main battle tanks. The Israelis now counter-attacked, opening a corridor between the Egyptian Second Army in the north and Third Army in the south. Pushing towards the Suez Canal via that corridor, Israeli troops crossed the Suez Canal and established a bridgehead on the west bank. This bold move eventually resulted in the Third Army being cut off from Egypt by war's end. The Israeli offensive simultaneously eliminated the Egyptian ADF threat, offering the IDF/AF a better opportunity to support ground forces. As the Egyptian high command began to realise the implications of the Israeli bridgehead, and of the ADF collapse, Egyptian air strikes intensified, providing a target-rich environment for the Israeli delta-fighters.

Menachem Sharon became an ace on 14 October, followed 48 hours later by Shlomo Levi, who was involved in two actions on this day;

'We flew over the IDF corridor. I looked down – what a mess, so many vehicles. Just as I thought to myself that any Egyptian attack aircraft would simply have to open fire and he would surely hit something, the controller ordered, "Elite, engage, 270. MiG-17s". There were eight MiG-17s in two four-ship formations at low altitude. We jettisoned our fuel tanks and turned right of the MiGs. I was amazed at how slowly they were flying – maybe 250 knots. The MiG-17's manoeuvrability at low altitude was fantastic, and it didn't have a G-meter at all – only a warning light that came on at 12G. But this didn't mean that it was the jet's limit. It simply meant that if the pilot was still able to see, then he was pulling 12G!

'I came in after a pair and they split. I chased one of them, flying roughly north-west. I opened fire and hit him. It was pouring smoke, but just before it hit the ground my wingman yelled, "One, pay attention behind you". I looked behind and there were two MiG-17s in close formation shooting at me. I was flying at just 180 knots and at less than 300 ft AGL. The MiGs could out-turn me, so my only escape option was to descend and accelerate, as they didn't have AAMs. I continued to turn until I was flying roughly south-east. Then I accelerated, but I felt that I was descending too much. I was close to hitting the ground.

'The MiG-17 had an interesting feature in that its cannon were angled upwards. Usually, when an aircraft opened fire you looked backwards and saw the belly of the pursuing fighter, but with the MiG-17 you saw the uppersurfaces due to the deflection of the cannon. I looked behind and

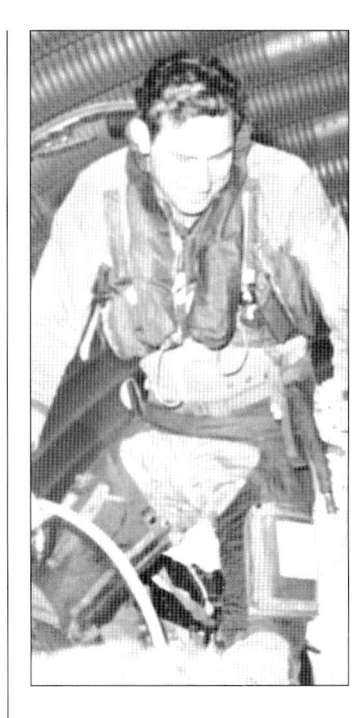

No 144 Sqn CO Menachem Sharon became an ace on 14 October 1973 when he destroyed two MiG-21s in Nesher 24

saw the flashes. I looked around and saw the explosions on the sand dunes. In the mirror I saw a huge explosion. I accelerated to 400 knots and began to turn left towards the combat area, where I saw no aircraft, only pillars of smoke. I got nearer and saw two crash paths on the ground. At the end of each were two wrecked MiG-17s. Either they didn't pay attention and had hit the ground or, as a result of the cannon deflection, they had unintentionally descended when they opened fire on me.'

The two MiG-17s were credited to No 113 Sqn as unit kills. In his third scramble from Refidim that day, Levi was again fighting MiG-17s. He recalled how, after just one turn, he was right on the tail of a MiG-17;

'I was right behind him. A cannon burst, a huge fireball and he crashed west of the canal. I couldn't see if there was an ejection, but there I was again at 240 knots, so I informed everybody, "Pay attention to your speed". I accelerated, just like in the morning, only this time I was not chased by two MiG-17s.

'I flew south-east, and when I reached 420 knots I started to turn west. At that moment I felt a huge bang and the aircraft rocked. All the warning lights came on – oil, alternator, everything. At the same time, I saw out of the corner of my eye a burning aircraft falling east of the Suez Canal. I hardly had any thrust, so I launched the two Shafrirs, activated the emergency engine control unit and set course for Refidim. I reported that I was hit and called my wingman, but he didn't answer.

On 18 October 1973, Shlomo Levi was scrambled from Hatzor in Nesher 18, with Amit Eshchar as his wingman. They were on their way to the Suez Canal when the ground controller radioed, 'Engage, 180 – 25 miles'. They jettisoned their external fuel tanks but saw nothing, and Levi was also hampered by a communication malfunction. He later recounted, 'Suddenly, we saw them – six (Libyan) Mirages jettisoning everything they had, including their bombs and tanks. Then one of them crashed into the water. We already had the yellow ID triangles, and their camouflage scheme was darker than ours. They saw us, and attempted to escape west, low over the sea. The sun was very low, and they were flying into it. At first Eshchar got too close behind a Mirage, so I said, "Step aside" and launched an AAM. I could barely see anything, but then there was an explosion – I had shot him down. Then I heard that an F-4 formation was also vectored to engage, and I was afraid of a friendly-fire incident. I saw Eshchar chasing a Mirage and ordered him to disengage. He said, "Just one moment" and launched an AAM. I couldn't look into the sun, but saw the silhouette of the missile on the water chasing the silhouette of the Mirage. Then the small silhouette impacted the large one and, puff, an explosion. I said, "Disengage" but he replied, "One more moment". I had already turned back when I heard him say, "Wow." I asked what had happened, and he replied, "An F-4 did a pass on me". Luckily, the Phantom II crews had identified him as friendly and didn't open fire. I've replayed that combat in my mind over and over again – we should have got all six Mirages. We should have shot them down one after the other like sitting ducks, but that's life. We shot down two, and a third volunteered.' The latter Mirage became a squadron kill

The wreckage of Shahak 19, photographed on 15 October 1973. The missing ejection seat may indicate that the pilot 'banged out', while the sign taped onto the battered fuselage reads, *Warning. Armed Aircraft*

'On finals, I saw a cleaning vehicle sweeping the runway. Just after we took-off, a damaged A-4 had landed and was stopped by the net, so the runway had to be cleaned. I yanked over it, touched down and then deployed the braking 'chute, but nothing happened. I asked the control tower to deploy the net and I was stopped just beside a AAA position. I opened the canopy, climbed out, walked away from the aircraft, maybe 20 or 30 m, and had a look – SA-7 hit.'

The next day Michael Zuk achieved ace status, while up north four No 117 Sqn Shahaks escorted F-4s that had been sent to bomb a Syrian bridge near Nabek. Yuval Ne'eman got three MiGs during the Yom Kippur War, but was far prouder of the two he failed to down.

'During the war I noticed that a young pilot was depressed. "What's the matter?" I asked. He answered, "The war will soon be over and I haven't got a MiG yet". I went to the operations room and saw there was a mission to Nabek, escorting F-4s. I asked to be leader of the four-ship formation, with that pilot as my wingman. I explained that this mission was up north where the Syrians had less advanced MiG-21s and less capable pilots, and that this was his chance to catch a MiG. We trailed the F-4s at low altitude, and as they pulled-up to bomb, we started to climb to the CAP altitude of 20,000 ft.

'We had nearly got there when No 3 yelled, "MiGs!" We turned, but saw nothing. I asked No 3, "Where are you?" He reported his position. It was pretty far away so I ordered him to return home, but just then I saw two MiG-21s below us. I said to my wingman, "Here are your MiGs". At first he didn't see them, so we turned 360 degrees until he did. He downed the first quite quickly, and then chased the other. I ordered him to disengage, but he kept chasing that MiG. I had no option but to turn back, while all the time ordering him to disengage – we were very low on fuel. Finally, after downing the second MiG, he reported that he was running out of fuel. I ordered him to fly west towards the sea, and when he was off Beirut at about 30,000 ft his engine flamed-out. He glided until he was off the Israeli coast, where he ejected. I was criticised for not showing more authority as a leader, but I'm very proud that he got his MiGs.'

Ten delta fighter pilots became aces during the last six days of the war. Down south on the Egyptian front, multi-bogey engagements improved kill prospects, and the Refidim alert was the centre of activity. In fact, all 12 kills credited to the Hatzor delta squadrons on 19 October were claimed by Refidim-based pilots. Meanwhile, three No 144 Sqn pilots downed six Egyptian MiG-21s, as Ariel Cohen recalled;

'We intercepted a four-ship formation of MiG-21s escorting attack aircraft. I was No 4, so I came in last. pulled-up and saw a MiG-21 disengaging. I seized the opportunity and dived after him, opening fire at about 300 m. Usually, you had to give the gunsight a second or so to

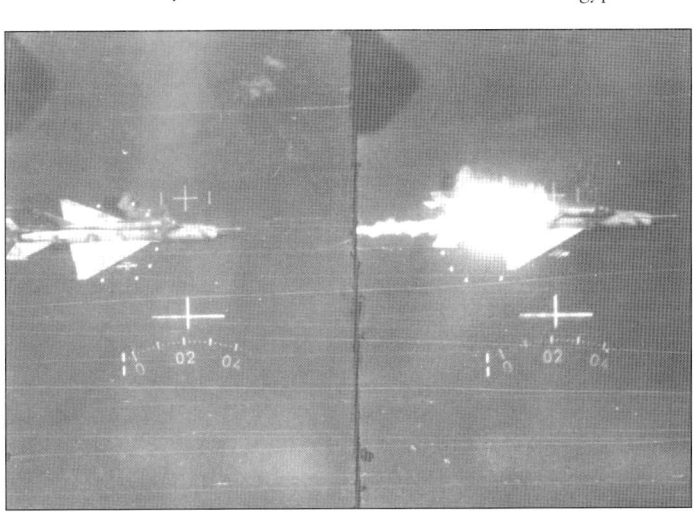

A MiG-21 leaves a trail of fire in its wake having been hit by cannon fire. This was the view afforded to an unnamed Shahak pilot during the Yom Kippur War

Perhaps the most spectacular kill ever filmed was this Egyptian MiG-21, shot down by Gidon Livni in Nesher 09 on 18 October 1973. The 5.5-kill ace claimed 2.5 of his victories on this day

stabilise on the target, but I placed the sight ahead of him. My estimate was correct, for the aircraft exploded and the pilot ejected. I rejoined my leader (Eli Menachem), by which time the MiG-21 formation had gone. Then another four-ship formation arrived. I followed my leader, who chased an aircraft which tried to perform a "split-S". The leader decided it was too risky so he let it go. But I was higher and followed the MiG. I finished the "split-S" right behind him, launched an AAM and the MiG exploded.'

The usual Egyptian strike pattern was to attack in the late afternoon when the sun was shining right in the Israeli fighter pilots' eyes, fly to Lake Bitter, turn north towards their target – the Deversoir bridgehead – and then head north-west back towards Egyptian territory. This pattern minimised the time and space available to the IDF/AF for interception, while the use of the 'train' tactic, with at least two four-ship formations flying in line astern, meant that any interceptors were caught in a 'sandwich'. It looked as though the Egyptians had learned a lesson or two from their repeated strikes on the bridgehead.

On 20 October an Egyptian ambush was set-up to trap Israeli interceptors. Just as four delta-fighters had intercepted Egyptian strike aircraft, and escorting fighters, additional MiG-21s – perhaps as many as ten pairs – popped-up from low altitude all over the area. Nevertheless, seven Egyptian jets were shot down, including four by Giora Epstein. He singlehandedly battled with ten MiG-21s after the remaining three Neshers had disengaged. Having claimed a MiG early on in the battle, Epstein had subsequently downed three more fighters. He was then amazed to find himself alone in the sky, all the MiG-21s having disappeared.

By 20 October Arab diplomats had finally agreed to discuss a cease-fire. But until it was implemented on the 24th, Israel intensified its activity to complete the siege of the Egyptian Third Army, and thus come to within 100 of Cairo. On the Syrian front, a local offensive was launched to re-capture Mount Hermon. Both efforts were successful, and resulted in air activity being stepped-up. Gidon Dror achieved ace status on the 23rd – a day he was to remember;

'We were vectored west of Suez City, flying at 25,000 ft at Mach 0.9 – the fastest speed possible with external tanks still full of fuel. We waited for further instructions, but they never came. As we passed Kotamiya air base, Cairo was visible on the horizon, but still nobody talked to us. Deep into Egypt, without ground control guidance, we were intercepted by MiG-21s. Each of us broke in a different direction and we started to fight for our lives. I engaged two shining MiG-21s, which looked as though they had just come off the production line. Luckily, they didn't split and didn't take advantage of their numerical superiority. I managed to use the vertical dimension better than them, so after four or five "stitches", I shot down the trailing MiG with a burst from my cannon. The leading one

IDF/AF CO Maj Gen Beni Peled (far right) is escorted by Hatzor base CO Amos Lapidot (partially obscured, to Peled's right) on a visit to No 113 Sqn during the Yom Kippur War. Also seen in this photo, in flying gear, are (from left to right) Gidon Dror, Shlomo Levi (junior deputy CO), Amos Shachar, Moshe Hertz (senior deputy CO) and Amit Eshchar. These five pilots were credited with 29 kills between them

Ra'anan Yosef used Refidim-based Nesher 10 to claim his second kill on 18 October 1973 when he shot down this Egyptian MiG-21. The aircraft's brake parachute was probably deployed as a result of the damage inflicted by Yosef's cannon fire. The starboard horizontal stabiliser also appears to be badly damaged. The Egyptian pilot ejected seconds later. This action is also depicted in the specially commissioned cover artwork for this volume

No 101 Sqn's Shahak 59 was damaged in a take-off accident on 7 October 1973, and it was not repaired until after the war had ended. The jet's pilot, Israel Baharav (the squadron's senior deputy CO), suffered severe burns to his right hand in the crash. He returned to flying only after becoming acting squadron boss in the wake of CO Avi Lanir's ejection over Syria on 13 October 1973. Flying with a bandaged hand, Baharav added three kills in the last two days of the war to the nine he had scored before the conflict

Israel Baharav was credited with his fifth, and last, double MiG-21 kill in Nesher 25 on 24 October 1973

No 101 Sqn's reconnaissance officer, Gidon Livni, was on vacation in the USA (along with No 144 Sqn pilot Amir Yahel and their wives) when the Yom Kippur War broke-out. He made it to Hatzor from Las Vegas in just two days, arriving on 8 October 1973. He flew 43 sorties between the 9th and the 24th, being credited with his first kill on the 17th

immediately dived to disengage. I launched an AAM, but it homed on the sand dunes. I was already low on fuel, so I didn't chase him.

'On my way back I saw two MiG-17s returning from the Suez Canal, and then two L-29s, but I restrained myself – I didn't have fuel for another engagement. Back at Refidim, I asked the ground controllers why they had ignored us. I was told that there had been problems with an engagement over Syria at the same time as our fight, so they concentrated on that, trusting that we would manage on our own!'

Over Syria, Israel Baharav was credited with his tenth kill while Kobi Richter reached 10.5 to join an exclusive group of Israeli double-figure aces. Before the Yom Kippur War, Asher Snir had been the group's sole member, but he was followed by Salmon on 8 October, Koren on the 16th, Epstein on the 19th and Levi on the 22nd. Additionally, Yiftach Spector, who was credited with eight kills as a Shahak pilot, became a

Once a year, on IDF/AF Day, kill certificates such as this one were awarded to victorious pilots. This example belongs to Dan Sever, and it was awarded for his victory over an Su-7 on 8 October 1973. In order to avoid criticism from those not flying interceptors, and to honour the efforts of other pilots in the air force, similar certificates indicating the number of operational sorties flown by each pilot in the past year were also awarded. Furthermore, during the Yom Kippur War, the traditional 'buzz' over home base following a kill was banned, as No 117 Sqn pilot Elisha Peri recalled. 'On 12 October we were scrambled east. We visually acquired a MiG-21 pulling-up, possibly to intercept us. We usually avoided chasing a single aircraft due to the possibility of a "sandwich", but we did indeed get into one. My wingman, Neuner, yelled, "Break", but I was aware of the danger so I reversed and saw the contrails of the four missiles that had been launched. Then he rolled over, did a "split-S" and headed north at low altitude. I aimed at his jet pipe, my missile acquiring the target. I launched and hit. I asked my wingman to report, and he said, "I shot one down one". We looked for other MiGs but saw nothing, so we returned. We did not buzz the base. We had stopped after two days or so, as it was unacceptable to celebrate when attack aircraft pilots suffered so much. In the debriefing it turned out that both my wingman and I had launched at the same MiG-21. But my missile hit first and Neuner's hit the fireball, so it was definitely my kill'

Flames enveloping his jet, an Egyptian MiG-21 pilot ejects (his parachute can just be seen streaming below the fighter) over the Israeli bridgehead on the west bank of the Suez Canal on 19 October 1973. During the last six hours of daylight, when the sun was setting in the west, Israeli interceptors were at a distinct disadvantage. A series of large Egyptian air strikes were launched, resulting in multi-bogey engagements. These dogfights were watched by Israeli troops on the ground, and no doubt acted as a significant morale booster for them

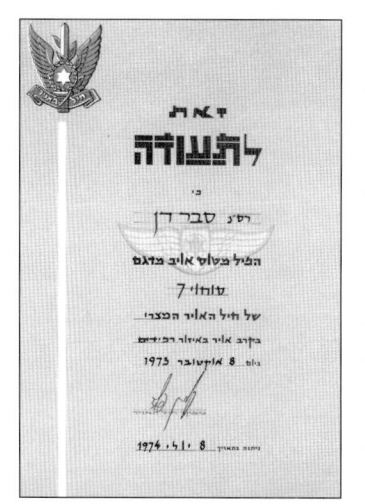

double-figure ace (with four more kills) during the Yom Kippur War whilst flying the F-4. All 14 victories credited to the delta fighter pilots on the war's last day were claimed in a single combat. Four Neshers from Refidim, led by Baharav, were the first to engage, and they were reinforced by four Shahaks from Hatzor, led by Epstein. The battle was then joined by a No 144 Sqn pair, led by Eli Menachem, who reported that they had almost finished their CAP and still had a lot of fuel, although not enough for air combat;

'We asked the controller for permission to join and he approved, so the leader ordered us to jettison external fuel tanks and activate afterburner. But I flew economically without afterburner and, indeed, after a minute or so my leader and his wingman turned back. I pressed on with my wingman. Far on the horizon we saw signs of air combat, and when we arrived the first thing I saw was a Shahak engulfed in flames. It was Epstein. He had suffered an engine compressor stall, which in the Mirage was indicated by a trail of fire. I immediately joined Epstein. It was a relief for him to be escorted, although I wasn't from his squadron. Seconds later we were on the same radio channel talking to each other.

'He switched off his engine, restarted and we returned to the combat together. Then a MiG-21 came right in front of us. He couldn't have seen us. His belly was pointed at us. I was starting to lick my lips because I noticed it was too close for Epstein, but ideal for me. Against all odds, Epstein launched an AAM and the missile didn't even manoeuvre. It simply flew like an arrow and hit the MiG-21! I then realised that I musn't fly close to Epstein because he shot down everything.

'I separated and flew alone without activating the afterburner in a sky full of fighters. I saw a Mirage and a MiG-21 in a scissors at really slow speed. I was flying relatively fast so I said, "The one in scissors, let go. I will take him". I pointed my gunsight at the MiG and when I was within range fired a short burst. I overtook the tremendous explosion at relative speed – I was flying at about 500 knots, while the MiG was doing 150.'

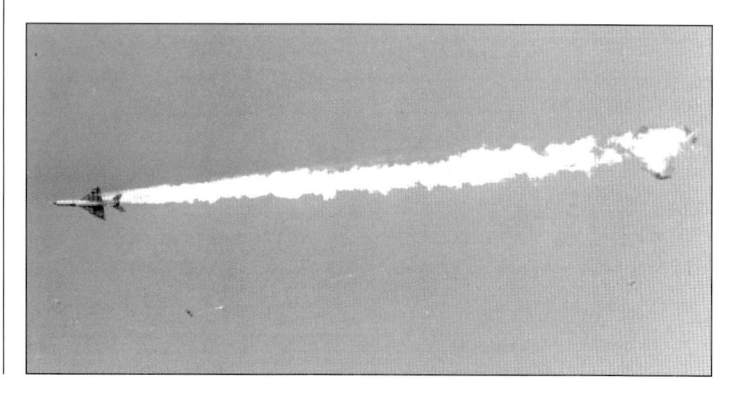

EPILOGUE

During the Yom Kippur War, 74 Israeli delta-fighter pilots flew nearly 3000 sorties in just 19 days. The average rate of sorties to engagements was over ten-to-one, meaning that a pilot who flew 50 missions could hope to participate in five combats. EP pilot Ra'anan Yosef of No 113 Sqn fought in five and shot down three aircraft, while No 144 Sqn reserve pilot Assaf Ben-Nun participated in four and shot down four, one during each encounter. More than a third of Israeli Yom Kippur War delta-fighter pilots became aces – a testimony to their high level of training and professionalism. Furthermore, only a fifth failed to shoot down enemy aircraft.

Although the overall number of kills is impressive, further analysis reveals an average of 11 kills per day, or 2.6 per squadron per day. Inevitably, the most successful pilots were those who were in the right place at the right time, and then exploited their opportunities to the full. Giora Epstein, the top scoring Israeli ace of all time, was involved in five engagements during which he shot down 12 enemy aircraft.

Fighting Mach 2 fighters using tactics derived from World War 2 was soon to become but a memory in the years after the Yom Kippur War.

The final four kills achieved by Israeli delta-winged fighters were scored in April 1974 by No 101 Sqn during skirmishes with the Syrians in the battle for control of Mount Hermon. On the 19th Avraham Salmon shot down two Syrian MiG-21s in Shahak No 58 to become the second highest scoring Israeli ace with 14.5 kills. Ten days later Gidon Livni became the last Israeli to become a delta-fighter ace when he shot down a Syrian MiG-21 in Nesher 78. As he later recalled, a pilot best remembers his misses, not his kills;

'In that combat I could have shot down three, but I wasn't lucky and so got just one. We patrolled for a long time, and we had almost exhausted our fuel, when we were ordered to engage at high altitude. We didn't have enough time to

Avraham Salmon (left) became the last Israeli fighter pilot to be credited with a kill while flying the Shahak when he shot down two Syrian MiG-21s in aircraft 58 on 19 April 1974. This took his personal score to 14.5 kills, making him the second highest scoring Israeli ace. He is seen here with fellow reserve pilot, and 'MiG-killer', Dan Sever

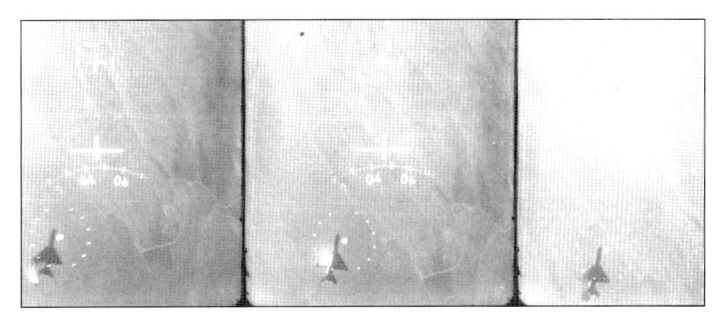

Gidon Livni became the last Israeli pilot to 'make ace' in a delta-fighter when he shot down a Syrian MiG-21 in Nesher 78 on 29 April 1974

These Neshers are seen being prepared for shipment to Argentina in the late 1970s. A total of 39 were exported to the South American country between 1978 and 1981

The Shahaks spent their twilight years with the IDF/AF operating from Eitham

Israel's top ace, Giora Epstein, finally retired from operational flying in May 1997. A reservist for 20 years, he had first flown the Shahak in 1966. Remaining in delta-fighters until 1988, he then converted onto the F-16, which he flew until his retirement

A unique gathering of veteran fighter pilots took place in Israel on 20 May 1997 to mark the retirement of Giora Epstein from operational flying at the age of 59. Pictured here, from left to right, are Eitan Ben-Eliyahu (IDF/AF CO 1996-2000), Ezer Weizman (IDF/AF CO 1958-1966 and Israeli President 1993-2000) and Epstein himself. In March 1965, Weizman awarded Epstein his wings, the latter having previously served as a paratrooper between 1956 and 1963, when he entered the IDF/AF Flying School as a cadet

accelerate. We jettisoned our external fuel tanks, but didn't come in fast enough. The MiGs above us were in a much better position tactically, but I still pulled-up, together with Bodinger. It was soon clear that we wouldn't have enough energy to complete the manoeuvre, however.

'Then I saw four other MiGs flying very fast at high altitude. I chased them until I was about 1000 m behind them, but I could get no closer. I launched an AAM but nothing happened. The MiG was in my sight but the missile didn't launch – very sad. They disappeared immediately afterwards. These were reconnaissance MiGs, and all the others we saw were their escorts. I descended, and I saw two in a right-hand turn, but I didn't know if they were MiGs or F-4s. I decided to close to cannon range – my AAMs didn't function in any case. I chased the trailing MiG. A single cannon burst and it caught fire. The pilot didn't eject, and it crashed into the ground.'

These last four kills took the number of victories credited to the Shahak and Nesher to a staggering 397.5 (282.5 for the Shahak and 115 for the Nesher) between 1966 and 1974, although the fluid nature of the history air warfare history means these figures can still change. What was not disputed was the fact that in the second half of the 1970s, a new generation of combat aircraft rendered the delta-fighters virtually obsolete. The Nesher was the first to be retired, while the Shahaks soldiered on until 1982 to complete 20 years of glorious service. They also fought in one more war, over Lebanon in June 1982. Avner Slapak was still flying the aircraft as a reserve pilot then, some 15 years after scoring the tenth Shahak kill. He could hardly fail to notice the way things had changed;

'We patrolled with the F-15s, and when we were vectored to engage they accelerated ahead of us until they disappeared in the distance. We could no longer see them, but continued to fly the course we were given. A few minutes later the F-15s returned, and the pilots told us how many kills they had got. It was then that I realised it wasn't our game any more.'

APPENDICES

SHAHAK/NESHER ACES

Pilot	Squadron/s	1962-67	Seven Day War	1967-73	Yom Kippur War to 1974	Additional kills	Total
Giora Epstein	101	-	1	4	12	-	17
Avraham Salmon	119, 101	-	2	6.5	6	-	14.5
Asher Snir	119	-	3	9	-	1.5 in F-4	13.5
Israel Baharav	101	-	-	9	3	-	12
Yiftach Spector	101	1.5	-	6.5	-	4 in F-4	12
Yehuda Koren	117	1	2	3.5	4	-	10.5
Kobi Richter	117	-	-	6.5	4	-	10.5
Shlomo Levi	101, 113	-	-	-	10	-	10
Oded Marom	101	-	1	6	2.5	-	9.5
Eitan Karmi	119, 101	-	2	2	5	-	9
Dror Harish	119, 101	-	-	4	5	-	9
Ilan Gonen	101, 113	-	1	2	5	-	8
Amos Bar	117	-	-	2	5	1 in F-16	8
Uri Gil	117	-	1	-	4.5	2 in F-16	7.5
Ran Ronen	119	2	2	3	-	-	7
Amos Amir	101, 119	-	1	6	-	-	7
Michael Zuk	101	-	-	2	5	-	7
Yermi Keidar	-	-	-	6	-	1 in Super Mystere	7
Moshe Hertz	101, 113	-	-	1	5.5	-	6.5
Yoram Agmon	101	1	-	1	-	4 in F-4	6
Uri Aven-Nir	117, 144	-	1	2	3	-	6
Menachem Sharon	101, 144	-	-	2	4	-	6
Eli Menachem	119, 144	-	-	1	5	-	6
Gidon Livni	101	-	-	-	5.5	-	5.5
Ezra Dotan	117	1	2	-	-	2 in A-4	5
Giora Rom	119	-	5	-	-	-	5
Menachem Shmul	119, 144	-	3	1	1	-	5
Reuven Rozen	119, 113	-	1	3	1	-	5
Gidon Dror	117, 113	-	1	-	4	-	5
Shlomo Navot	117	-	-	5	-	-	5
Ithamar Neuner	119, 117	-	-	4	1	-	4
Avraham Gilad	119, 113	-	-	2	3	-	5
Yoram Geva	119, 101	-	-	2	3	-	5
Ariel Cohen	144	-	-	-	5	-	5
Assaf Ben-Nun	144	-	-	-	4	1 in Mystere	5

SHAHAK/NESHER KILL/LOSS RATES and WEAPONS USED

Timeframe	Kills-to-Losses[1]	Weapons Used
July 1966 to April 1967	11-to-1	10 cannon, 1 Yahalom
Six Day War	50.5-to-4	47 cannon, 0.5 Shafrir, 3 no weapon
July 1967 to February 1969	11-to-1	9 cannon, 2 Shafrir
March to December 1969	44-to-3	33 cannon, 1 Shafrir, 1 AIM-9, 8 Shafrir 2, 1 no weapon
1970	52-to-4	27 cannon, 12 AIM-9, 8 Shafrir 2, 5 no weapon
September 1972 to September 1973	14-to-1	8 AIM-9, 5 Shafrir 2, 1 cannon
Yom Kippur War	211[2]-to-11	101 Sqn – 15.5 Shafrir 2, 12 AIM-9, 27 cannon, 3 no weapon
		113 Sqn – 11 Shafrir 2, 13.5 cannon, 8 no weapon, 24.5 unknown
		117 Sqn – 14 Shafrir 2, 6 cannon, 1 slipstream, 7 no weapon, 26.5 unknown
		144 Sqn – 23 Shafrir 2, 15 cannon, 4 no weapon
April 1974	4-to-0	2 AIM-9, 2 cannon

Notes
1 – Air combat losses
2 – Incomplete data

SHAHAK/NESHER VICTORIES

Date	Squadron	Pilot	Aircraft	Kill	Weapon
14/7/66	101	Agmon Yoram	Shahak 59	SAF MiG-21	Cannon
15/8/66	117	Koren Yehuda	Shahak 25	SAF MiG-21	Cannon
13/11/66	119	Ronen Ran	Shahak 84	RJAF Hunter	Cannon
29/11/66	101	Haber Michael	Shahak 34	EAF MiG-19	Cannon
29/11/66	101	Haber Michael	Shahak 34	EAF MiG-19	R.530
7/4/67	119	Ronen Ran	Shahak	SAF MiG-21	Cannon
7/4/67	101	Slapak Avner	Shahak81	SAF MiG-21	Cannon
7/4/67	117	Dotan Ezra	Shahak	SAF MiG-21	Cannon
7/4/67	117	Lanir Abraham	Shahak 60	SAF MiG-21	Cannon
7/4/67	101	Romach Binyamin	Shahak 57	SAF MiG-21 (0.5)	Cannon
7/4/67	101	Spector Yiftach	Shahak 52	SAF MiG-21	Cannon
7/4/67	101	Spector Yiftach	Shahak 52	SAF MiG-21 (0.5)	Cannon
5/6/67	101	Sever Dan	Shahak 77	EAF MiG-21	No weapon
5/6/67	101	Gonen Ilan	Shahak 59	EAF Il-14	Cannon
5/6/67	119	Karmi Eitan	Shahak 03?	EAF MiG-21	Cannon
5/6/67	119	Karmi Eitan	Shahak 03?	EAF MiG-21	Cannon
5/6/67	119	Rom Giora	Shahak 66	EAF MiG-21	Cannon
5/6/67	119	Rom Giora	Shahak 66	EAF MiG-21	Cannon
5/6/67	119	Levoshin Arnon	Shahak 20?	EAF MiG-19	Cannon
5/6/67	119	Ronen Ran	Shahak	EAF MiG-19	Cannon
5/6/67	119	Ronen Ran	Shahak	EAF MiG-19	Cannon
5/6/67	119	No 119 Sqn	-	EAF MiG-19	No weapon
5/6/67	119	Sagi Oded	Shahak 44?	RJAF Hunter	Cannon
5/6/67	119	Rom Giora	Shahak 43	SAF MiG-21	Cannon
5/6/67	119	Snir Asher	Shahak 32	SAF MiG-21	Cannon
5/6/67	117	Gil Uri	Shahak	SAF MiG-21	Cannon
5/6/67	117	Arad Amnon	Shahak	SAF MiG-17	Cannon
5/6/67	117	Arad Amnon	Shahak	SAF MiG-17	Cannon
5/6/67	117	Aven-Nir Uri	Shahak 45	IrAF Hunter	Cannon
5/6/67	117	Dotan Ezra	Shahak	SAF MiG-21	Cannon
5/6/67	117	Henkin Ehud	Shahak 42	SAF MiG-21	Cannon
6/6/67	101	Barzilai Yitzhak	Shahak 73	EAF Su-7	Cannon
6/6/67	101	Epstein Giora	Shahak 56	EAF Su-7	Cannon
6/6/67	101	Friedman Baruch	Shahak 06	EAF Su-7	Cannon
6/6/67	101	Ran Avshalom	Shahak 77	EAF Su-7	Cannon
6/6/67	119	Sagi Oded	Shahak 03	EAF Su-7	Cannon
6/6/67	119	Afek Omri	Shahak 20	EAF MiG-19	Cannon
6/6/67	119	Sagi Oded	Shahak 66	EAF MiG-19	Cannon
6/6/67	101	Furman Giora	Shahak 81	EAF MiG-21	Cannon
6/6/67	119	Yeari Uri	Shahak 03	EAF MiG-21	Cannon
6/6/67	101	Marom Oded	Shahak 15	EAF MiG-19	Cannon
6/6/67	101	Shachar Uri	Shahak 59	EAF MiG-19	Cannon
6/6/67	117	Arad Amnon	Shahak	IrAF Tu-16 (0.5)	Shafrir
6/6/67	117	Koren Yehuda	Shahak 45	IrAF Hunter	Cannon
6/6/67	117	Koren Yehuda	Shahak 45	IrAF MiG-21	Cannon
7/6/67	117	Dotan Ezra	Shahak	IrAF Hunter	Cannon
7/6/67	117	Dror Gidon	Shahak 60	IrAF Hunter	Cannon
7/6/67	101	Amir Amos	Shahak 09	EAF MiG-19	Cannon
7/6/67	101	Richter Yochai	Shahak 34	EAF MiG-19	Cannon
7/6/67	101	No 101 Sqn	-	EAF MiG-19	No weapon
7/6/67	119	Rom Giora	Shahak 41	EAF MiG-17	Cannon
7/6/67	119	Rom Giora	Shahak 41	EAF MiG-17	Cannon
8/6/67	101	Lev Arlozor	Shahak 33	EAF MiG-17	Cannon
8/6/67	119	Salmon Abraham	Shahak 68	EAF MiG-19	Cannon
8/6/67	119	Salmon Abraham	Shahak 68	EAFMiG-19	Cannon
8/6/67	119	Shmul Menachem	Shahak	EAF MiG-19	Cannon
8/6/67	119	Shmul Menachem	Shahak	EAF Il-28	Cannon
8/6/67	119	Shmul Menachem	Shahak	EAF MiG-21	Cannon
8/6/67	101	Arazi Yosef	Shahak 15	EAF MiG-21	Cannon
8/6/67	119	Rozen Reuven	Shahak 58	EAF MiG-17	Cannon
9/6/67	119	Snir Asher	Shahak 7x	EAF MiG-17	Cannon
9/6/67	119	Snir Asher	Shahak 7x	EAF MiG-17	Cannon
9/6/67	117	Henkin Ehud	Shahak	SAF MiG-21	?
8/7/67	119	Ben-Nun Avihu	Shahak 41	EAF MiG-21	Cannon
15/7/67	119	Snir Asher	Shahak	EAF MiG-17	Cannon
15/7/67	119	Snir Asher	Shahak	EAF MiG-17	Cannon
15/7/67	101	Agmon Yoram	Shahak 81	EAF Su-7	Cannon

Date	Squadron	Pilot	Aircraft	Kill	Weapon
15/7/67	119	Prigat Eliezer	Shahak 68	EAF MiG-21	Cannon
15/7/67	119	Ronen Ran	Shahak 83?	EAF MiG-21	Shafrir
10/10/67	119	Ben-Nun Avihu	Shahak 32	EAF MiG-21	Cannon
12/10/68	101	Marom Oded	Shahak 81	EAF MiG-21	Cannon
12/2/69	117	Liss Uri	Shahak	SAF MiG-21	Shafrir?
24/2/69	101	Shamir Amnon	Shahak 56	SAF MiG-21	Cannon
24/2/69	117	Richter Yaacov	Shahak	SAF MiG-17	Cannon
8/3/69	101	Zuk Michael	Shahak 14	EAF MiG-21	Cannon
14/4/69	119	Rozen Reuven	Shahak 68	EAF MiG-21	AIM-9B
21/5/69	119	Ronen Ran	Shahak 03?	EAF MiG-21	Cannon
21/5/69	119	Rozen Reuven	Shahak 58	EAF MiG-21	Cannon
21/5/69	119	Snir Asher	Shahak 68?	EAF MiG-21	Cannon
29/5/69	117	Nuener Ithamar	Shahak	SAF MiG-21	Shafrir
24/6/69	119	Amir Amos	Shahak 19	EAF MiG-21	Cannon
26/6/69	101	Spector Yiftach	Shahak 33	EAF MiG-21	Cannon
26/6/69	119	Snir Asher	Shahak 6x	EAF MiG-21	AIM-9B
2/7/69	119	Amir Amos	Shahak 68	EAF MiG-21	Cannon
2/7/69	119	Karmi Eitan	Shahak 58?	EAF MiG-21	AIM-9B
2/7/69	119	Karmi Eitan	Shahak 58?	EAF MiG-21	Cannon
2/7/69	117	Richter Yaacov	Shahak	EAF MiG-21	Shafrir 2
7/7/69	101	Keldes Avinoam	Shahak 07	EAF MiG-21	No weapon
7/7/69	101	Marom Oded	Shahak 59	EAF MiG-21	Cannon
8/7/69	101	Ben-Eliyahu Eitan	Shahak 33	SAF MiG-21	Cannon
8/7/69	101	Furman Giora	Shahak 56	SAF MiG-21	Cannon
8/7/69	101	Furman Giora	Shahak 56	SAF MiG-21	Cannon
8/7/69	117	Goren Ran	Shahak	SAF MiG-21	Shafrir 2
8/7/69	117	Aven-Nir Uri	Shahak	SAF MiG-21	Shafrir 2
8/7/69	117	Navot Shlomo	Shahak	SAF MiG-21	Shafrir 2
8/7/69	117	Richter Yaacov	Shahak	SAF MiG-21	Cannon
20/7/69	101	Epstein Giora	Shahak 82	EAF MiG-17	Cannon
20/7/69	101	Spector Yiftach	Shahak 52	EAF MiG-21	Cannon
20/7/69	101	Yoeli Giora	Shahak 59	EAF MiG-17	Cannon
24/7/69	101	Gordon Shamuel	Shahak 82	EAF Su-7	Cannon
24/7/69	101	Zuk Michael	Shahak 07	EAF Su-7	Cannon
24/7/69	117	Navot Shlomo	Shahak	EAF MiG-21	Shafrir 2
24/7/69	117	Goren Ran	Shahak	EAF Su-7	Cannon
11/9/69	117	Navot Shlomo	Shahak	EAF MiG-21	Cannon
11/9/69	101	Epstein Giora	Shahak 59	EAF Su-7	Cannon
11/9/69	101	Gonen Ilan	Shahak 82	EAF Su-7	Cannon
11/9/69	117	Friedman Avshalom	Shahak	EAF MiG-21	Cannon
11/9/69	117	Koren Yehuda	Shahak 50	EAF MiG-21	Shafrir 2
11/9/69	119	Harish Dror	Shahak 32?	EAF MiG-21	Cannon
11/9/69	119	Snir Asher	Shahak 6x	EAF MiG-21	Cannon
6/10/69	101	Baharav Israel	Shahak 82	EAF MiG-21	Cannon
6/10/69	101	Baharav Israel	Shahak 82	EAF MiG-21	Cannon
6/10/69	101	Marom Oded	Shahak 81	EAF MiG-21	Cannon
11/11/69	101	Sela Yair	Shahak 59	EAF MiG-21	Cannon
11/11/69	101	Sharon Menachem	Shahak 82	EAF MiG-21	Cannon
27/11/69	117	Navot Shlomo	Shahak	EAF MiG-21	Shafrir 2
11/12/69	117	Aven-Nir Uri	Shahak	SAF MiG-21	Shafrir 2
11/12/69	119	Nir Yitzhak	Shahak 83	SAF MiG-17	Cannon
11/12/69	119	Shmul Menachem	Shahak 58	SAF MiG-17	Cannon
4/1/70	101	Marom Oded	Shahak 59	EAF MiG-21	Cannon
4/1/70	117	Nuener Ithamar	Shahak	EAF MiG-21	Shafrir 2
8/1/70	117	Navot Shlomo	Shahak	SAF MiG-21	No weapon
8/1/70	117	Nuener Ithamar	Shahak	SAF MiG-21	Cannon
8/1/70	117	Richter Yaacov	Shahak	SAF MiG-21	Shafrir 2
8/2/70	119	Salmon Abraham	Shahak 80	EAF MiG-21	Cannon
9/2/70	101	Keldes Avinoam	Shahak 57	EAF MiG-21	Cannon
26/2/70	119	Amir Amos	Shahak 58	EAF MiG-21	Cannon
26/2/70	119	Gilad Abraham	Shahak 32	EAF MiG-21	Cannon
26/2/70	119	Salmon Abraham	Shahak 83	EAF MiG-21	Cannon
6/3/70	101	Spector Yiftach	Shahak 59	EAF MiG-21	Cannon
16/3/70	101	Sharon Menachem	Shahak 77	EAF MiG-21	No weapon
25/3/70	101	Baharav Israel	Shahak 81	EAF MiG-21	Cannon
25/3/70	101	Epstein Giora	Shahak 77	EAF MiG-21	Cannon
25/3/70	101	Epstein Giora	Shahak 77	EAF MiG-21	Cannon
25/3/70	101	Marom Oded	Shahak 15	EAF MiG-21	AIM-9B
27/3/70	101	Baharav Israel	Shahak 52	EAF MiG-21	AIM-9B/E

Date	Squadron	Pilot	Aircraft	Kill	Weapon
27/3/70	101	Baharav Israel	Shahak 52	EAF MiG-21	Cannon
27/3/70	119	Levoshin Arnon	Shahak 83	EAF MiG-21	No weapon
27/3/70	119	Snir Asher	Shahak	EAF MiG-21	Cannon
27/3/70	119	Snir Asher	Shahak	EAF MiG-21	Cannon
2/4/70	119	Amir Amos	Shahak 58	SAF MiG-21	AIM-9B
2/4/70	119	Gilad Abraham	Shahak 83	SAF MiG-21	No weapon
2/4/70	119	Salmon Abraham	Shahak 68	SAF MiG-21	Cannon
25/4/70	119	Amir Amos	Shahak 58	EAF Il-28	AIM-9E
28/4/70	119	Harish Dror	Shahak 83	EAF Su-7	AIM-9E
28/4/70	119	Nir Yitzhak	Shahak 79	EAF Su-7	Cannon
12/5/70	119	Snir Asher	Shahak 19	SAF MiG-17	AIM-9B
14/5/70	119	Amir Amos	Shahak 83	EAF MiG-21	Cannon
14/5/70	119	Rozen Reuven	Shahak 80	EAF MiG-21	AIM-9B
15/5/70	117	Richter Yaacov	Shahak	EAF MiG-17	AAM
15/5/70	117	Richter Yaacov	Shahak	EAF MiG-17	AAM
15/5/70	117	Koren Yehuda	Shahak 64	EAF MiG-21	Shafrir 2
16/5/70	119	Afek Omri	Shahak 85	EAF MiG-21	Cannon
16/5/70	119	Salmon Abraham	Shahak 68	EAF MiG-21	AIM-9E
3/6/70	117	Nuener Ithamar	Shahak	EAF MiG-21	Shafrir 2
3/6/70	119	Harish Dror	Shahak 4x	EAF MiG-21	Cannon
3/6/70	119	Harish Dror	Shahak 4x	EAF MiG-21	No weapon
3/6/70	119	Ronen Ran	Shahak 19	EAF MiG-21	Cannon
26/6/70	117	Koren Yehuda	Shahak 53	SAF MiG-21	Shafrir 2
26/6/70	117	Koren Yehuda	Shahak 47	SAF MiG-17 (0.5)	Cannon
26/6/70	117	Richter Yaacov	Shahak	SAF MiG-17 (0.5)	Cannon
26/6/70	117	Rokeach Amichai	Shahak	SAF MiG-17	Shafrir 2
27/6/70	119	Menachem Eliyahu	Shahak	EAF Mi-4	Cannon
10/7/70	101	Baharav Israel	Shahak 59	EAF MiG-21	AIM-9B
10/7/70	101	Baharav Israel	Shahak 59	EAF MiG-21	Cannon
10/7/70	101	Hertz Moshe	Shahak 15	EAF MiG-21	Cannon
10/7/70	101	Spector Yiftach	Shahak 52	EAF MiG-21	Cannon
27/7/70	101	Spector Yiftach	Shahak 34	EAF MiG-17	Cannon
27/7/70	101	Spector Yiftach	Shahak 34	EAF MiG-17	AIM-9D
30/7/70	101	Spector Yiftach	Shahak 52	USSR MiG-21 (0.5)	AIM-9D
30/7/70	119	Salmon Abraham	Shahak 78	USSR MiG-21 (0.5)	AIM-9D
30/7/70	119	Salmon Abraham	Shahak 78	USSR MiG-21	AIM-9D
30/7/70	119	Snir Asher	Shahak 6x	USSR MiG-21	AIM-9D
9/9/72	101	Auerbuch Ilan	Shahak 44	SAF Su-7	AIM-9D
9/9/72	101	Geva Yoram	Shahak 78	SAF Su-7	AIM-9D
9/11/72	101	Gonen Ilan	Shahak 51	SAF MiG-21	AIM-9D
9/11/72	101	Lanir Abraham	Shahak 78	SAF MiG-21	AIM-9D
21/11/72	117	Neeman Yuval	Shahak	SAF MiG-21	Shafrir 2
21/11/72	117	Vered Zvi	Shahak 79	SAF MiG-21	Shafrir 2
21/11/72	117	Meir Ran	Shahak	SAF MiG-21	Shafrir 2
8/1/73	101	Geva Yoram	Nesher 16	SAF MiG-21	AIM-9D
8/1/73	101	Yeari Eliezer	Nesher 10	SAF MiG-21	AIM-9D
13/9/73	101	Baharav Israel	Shahak 78	SAF MiG-21	Cannon
13/9/73	101	Baharav Israel	Shahak 78	SAF MiG-21	AIM-9D
13/9/73	101	Salmon Abraham	Shahak 59	SAF MiG-21	AIM-9D
13/9/73	117	Bar Amos	Shahak 79	SAF MiG-21	Shafrir 2
13/9/73	117	Bar Amos	Shahak 79	SAF MiG-21	Shafrir 2
6/10/73	144	Ben-Nun Assaf	Nesher 15	EAF Su-7	Shafrir 2
6/10/73	144	Keidar Yermiyahu	Nesher	EAF Su-7	Cannon
6/10/73	144	Keidar Yermiyahu	Nesher	EAF Su-7	Shafrir 2
6/10/73	144	Shmul Menachem	Nesher 03	EAF Su-7	Cannon
6/10/73	101	Karmi Eitan	Shahak 59	EAF AS-5	Cannon
6/10/73	113	Gilad Abraham	Nesher	EAF Mi-8	?
6/10/73	113	Gilad Abraham	Nesher	EAF Mi-8	?
6/10/73	117	Bar Amos	Shahak	SAF MiG-21	AAM
7/10/73	101	Karmi Eitan	Shahak 85?	EAF MiG-21	Shafrir 2
7/10/73	113	Tavor David	Nesher 93	EAF MiG-21	?
7/10/73	117	Friedman Avshalom	Shahak	SAF MiG-21	AAM
7/10/73	117	Friedman Avshalom	Shahak	SAF MiG-21	Cannon
7/10/73	117	Lahav Ami	Shahak 32	SAF MiG-21	?
7/10/73	117	Lahav Ami	Shahak	SAF MiG-21	?
7/10/73	117	Neeman Yuval	Shahak	SAF MiG-21	Cannon
7/10/73	117	Neeman Yuval	Shahak	SAF MiG-21	Shafrir 2
7/10/73	117	Richter Yaacov	Shahak	SAF MiG-21	?
7/10/73	117	Shlaider Daniel	Shahak	SAF MiG-21	?

Date	Squadron	Pilot	Aircraft	Kill	Weapon
7/10/73	117	Vered Zvi	Shahak 07	SAF MiG-21	Cannon
8/10/73	144	Kelman Shimcha	Nesher	EAF MiG-17	Shafrir 2
8/10/73	144	Kelman Shimcha	Nesher	EAF MiG-17	Shafrir 2
8/10/73	144	Sharon Menachem	Nesher 28	EAF MiG-17	Shafrir 2
8/10/73	101	Marom Oded	Shahak 58	SAF MiG-17	Shafrir 2
8/10/73	101	Katz Michael	Nesher 36	EAF Su-7	Shafrir 2
8/10/73	101	Sever Dan	Nesher 17	EAF Su-7	Shafrir 2
8/10/73	101	No 101 Sqn	-	EAF Su-7	No weapon
8/10/73	101	Zuk Michael	Nesher 65	EAF Su-7	AIM-9D
8/10/73	144	Cohen Ariel	Nesher	SAF Su-20	Shafrir 2
8/10/73	144	Goren Giora	Nesher	SAF Su-20	?
8/10/73	144	Ben-Nun Assaf	Nesher 12	EAF MiG-21	Cannon
8/10/73	144	Sharon Menachem	Nesher 03	EAF MiG-21	Cannon
8/10/73	101	Karmi Eitan	Nesher 93	EAF MiG-21	Cannon
8/10/73	101	Karmi Eitan	Nesher 93	EAF MiG-21	Shafrir 2
8/10/73	101	Marom Oded	Shahak 85?	IrAF Hunter	Cannon
8/10/73	101	Salmon Abraham	Shahak 19?	IrAF Hunter	Shafrir 2
8/10/73	101	Salmon Abraham	Shahak 19?	IrAF Hunter	Shafrir 2
8/10/73	101	Sheffer Yehoshoa	Nesher 10	EAF MiG-21	AIM-9D
8/10/73	113	Ben-Amitai Ehud	Nesher	EAF MiG-21	?
9/10/73	101	Harish Dror	Shahak 52	SAF MiG-17	cannon
9/10/73	101	Harish Dror	Shahak 52	SAF MiG-17	Shafrir 2
9/10/73	117	No 117 Sqn	-	SAF Mi-8	Slipstream
9/10/73	117	Vered Zvi	Shahak 79	SAF Mi-8	Cannon
9/10/73	117	Bodinger Hertzel	Shahak	SAF MiG-17	?
9/10/73	117	Liss Uri	Shahak	SAF Su-7	?
9/10/73	117	Richter Yochai	Shahak	SAF MiG-21 or Su-20	?
9/10/73	117	Shlaider Daniel	Shahak	SAF MiG-21	?
9/10/73	117	No 117 Sqn	-	SAF Su-20	No weapon
10/10/73	101	Marom Oded	Shahak 51	SAF Su-7 (0.5)	AIM-9D/G
10/10/73	117	Gil Uri	Shahak 83	SAF Su-7 (0.5)	?
10/10/73	113	Shachar Amos	Nesher 06	EAF MiG-17	?
10/10/73	113	Ben-Amitai Ehud	Nesher	EAF Su-7	?
10/10/73	113	No 113 Sqn	-	EAF Su-7	No weapon
10/10/73	117	Avneri Dror	Shahak	SAF MiG-17	AAM
10/10/73	117	Bar Amos	Shahak	SAF MiG-17	?
10/10/73	117	Gil Uri	Shahak	SAF Su-7	?
10/10/73	117	Koren Yehuda	Shahak 07	SAF MiG-17	AAM
10/10/73	117	Neeman Yuval	Shahak	SAF Su-7	Shafrir 2
10/10/73	117	Richter Yaacov	Shahak	SAF MiG-21	?
10/10/73	117	Richter Yochai	Shahak	SAF Su-7	?
10/10/73	117	No 117 Sqn	-	SAF MiG-17	No weapon
11/10/73	101	Neeman Raanan	Nesher 31	EAF MiG-21	Shafrir 2
11/10/73	101	Salmon Abraham	Nesher 10	EAF MiG-21	Cannon
11/10/73	113	Tavor David	Nesher 01	EAF MiG-21	Cannon
12/10/73	117	Peri Elisha	Shahak	SAF MiG-21	Shafrir 2
12/10/73	117	Seeon Dan	Shahak	SAF Su-7/20	AAM
12/10/73	117	Peri Elisha	Shahak	SAF MiG-21	Shafrir 2
12/10/73?	117	Shlaider Daniel	Shahak	SAF MiG-17	Shafrir 2
12/10/73	113	Levi Shlomo	Nesher 21	SAF Su-7	Cannon
12/10/73	113	Levi Shlomo	Nesher 21	SAF Su-7	Shafrir 2
12/10/73	113	Levi Shlomo	Nesher 21	SAF Su-7	Shafrir 2
12/10/73	117	Bar Amos	Shahak	SAF MiG-17	?
12/10/73	117	Bar Amos	Shahak	SAF MiG-21	?
12/10/73	117	Gil Uri	Shahak	SAF MiG-17 or 21	AAM
12/10/73	117	Gil Uri	Shahak	SAF MiG-17	AAM
12/10/73	117	Livni Amit	Shahak	SAF Su-7	?
12/10/73	117	Nuener Ithamar	Shahak	SAF Su-7	?
12/10/73	117	Rokeach Amichai	Shahak 83	SAF MiG-17	?
12/10/73	117	No 117 Sqn	-	SAF MiG-17	No weapon
13/10/73	113	Hertz Moshe	Nesher	SAF MiG-21	Shafrir 2
13/10/73	113	Rozen Reuven	Nesher 14	SAF Su-7	Cannon
13/10/73	113	No 113 Sqn	-	SAF MiG-21	No weapon
13/10/73	113	Yosef Raanan	Nesher 20	SAF MiG-17	Shafrir 2
13/10/73	117	Koren Yehuda	Shahak 66	SAF MiG-17	AAM
13/10/73	117	Koren Yehuda	Shahak 71	SAF Su-7	AAM
13/10/73	117	Seeon Dan	Shahak	SAF MiG-21	?
13/10/73	117	Seeon Dan	Shahak	SAF MiG-21	?
14/10/73	144	Ben-Nun Assaf	Nesher 33	EAF MiG-21	Cannon

APPENDICES

Date	Squadron	Pilot	Aircraft	Kill	Weapon
14/10/73	144	Lavi Yosef	Nesher	EAF MiG-21	Shafrir 2
14/10/73	144	Sharon Menachem	Nesher 24	EAF MiG-21	Cannon
14/10/73	144	Sharon Menachem	Nesher 24	EAF MiG-21	Shafrir 2
16/10/73	113	Levi Shlomo	Nesher 10	EAF MiG-17	Cannon
16/10/73	113	No 113 Sqn	-	EAF MiG-17	No weapon
16/10/73	113	No 113 Sqn	-	EAF MiG-17	No weapon
16/10/73	144	Cohen Ariel	Nesher	EAF MiG-17	Shafrir 2
16/10/73	144	Yahel Amir	Nesher	EAF MiG-17	Shafrir 2
16/10/73	101	Geva Yoram	Shahak 51	SAF Su-7	AIM-9G
16/10/73	101	Sever Dan	Nesher 10/31	EAF MiG-21	Shafrir 2
16/10/73	113	Eshchar Amit	Nesher	EAF MiG-21	?
16/10/73	113	Eshchar Amit	Nesher	EAF MiG-21	?
16/10/73	144	Keidar Yermiyahu	Nesher	EAF MiG-21/Su-7	Shafrir 2
16/10/73	113	Gonen Ilan	Nesher	EAF MiG-17	Cannon
16/10/73	113	Levi Shlomo	Nesher 14	EAF MiG-17	Cannon
16/10/73	113	No 113 Sqn	-	EAF MiG-17	No weapon
16/10/73	113	Gal Yaacov	Nesher	EAF Su-7	?
16/10/73	117	Bar Amos	Shahak	SAF Su-7	?
16/10/73	117	Koren Yehuda	Shahak 71	SAF MiG-21	AAM
16/10/73	117	Liss Uri	Shahak	SAF Su-7	?
17/10/73	101	Livni Gidon	Shahak 52	EAF MiG-21	Cannon
17/10/73	101	Zuk Michael	Shahak 58	EAF MiG-21	Cannon
17/10/73	113	Shachar Amos	Nesher	EAF MiG-21	?
17/10/73	113	Aderes Eitan	Nesher	EAF MiG-21	?
17/10/73	113	Ben-Amitai Ehud	Nesher	SAF MiG-21	?
17/10/73	113	No 113 Sqn	-	EAF MiG-21	No weapon
17/10/73	113	No 113 Sqn	-	SAF MiG-21	No weapon
17/10/73	117	Adar Eliezer	Shahak 14	SAF MiG-21	Cannon
17/10/73	117	Adar Eliezer	Shahak 14	SAF MiG-21	Cannon
18/10/73	101	Zuk Michael	Shahak 86	EAF Su-7/20	Cannon
18/10/73	113	Dror Gidon	Nesher	EAF MiG-17	Cannon
18/10/73	113	Dror Gidon	Nesher	EAF MiG-17	Cannon
18/10/73	101	Harish Dror	Nesher 65	EAF MiG-21	Cannon
18/10/73	101	Harish Dror	Nesher 65	EAF MiG-17	Shafrir 2
18/10/73	101	Livni Gidon	Nesher 09	EAF MiG-21 (0.5)	Cannon
18/10/73	101	Livni Gidon	Nesher 09	EAF MiG-21	Cannon
18/10/73	101	Livni Gidon	Nesher 09	EAF MiG-17	Shafrir 2
18/10/73	101	No 101 Sqn	-	EAF MiG-21	No weapon
18/10/73	113	Hertz Moshe	Nesher	EAF MiG-21 (0.5)	Cannon
18/10/73	113	Yosef Raanan	Nesher 10	EAF MiG-21	Cannon
18/10/73	101	Epstein Giora	Shahak 11	EAF Mi-8	Cannon
18/10/73	113	Eshchar Amit	Nesher	LARAF Mirage	Shafrir 2
18/10/73	113	Levi Shlomo	Nesher 18	LARAF Mirage	Shafrir 2
18/10/73	113	No 113 Sqn	-	LARAF Mirage	No weapon
19/10/73	101	No 101 Sqn	-	EAF MiG-17	No weapon
19/10/73	101	Harish Dror	Nesher 31	EAF MiG-21	Cannon
19/10/73	113	Hertz Moshe	Nesher	EAF MiG-21	?
19/10/73	101	Epstein Giora	Nesher 61	EAF Su-7	Cannon
19/10/73	101	Epstein Giora	Nesher 61	EAF Su-7	Shafrir 2
19/10/73	144	Aven-Nir Uri	Nesher	EAF MiG-21	?
19/10/73	144	Aven-Nir Uri	Nesher	EAF MiG-21	?
19/10/73	144	Cohen Ariel	Nesher	EAF MiG-21	Cannon
19/10/73	144	Cohen Ariel	Nesher	EAF MiG-21	Shafrir 2
19/10/73	144	Menachem Eliyahu	Nesher 24	EAF MiG-21	AAM
19/10/73	144	Menachem Eliyahu	Nesher 24	EAF MiG-21	Cannon
19/10/73	101	Epstein Giora	Nesher 61	EAF Su-20	Cannon
19/10/73	101	Epstein Giora	Nesher 61	EAF Su-20	Shafrir 2
19/10/73	101	Livni Gidon	Nesher 09	EAF Su-20	Cannon
19/10/73	113	Dror Gidon	Nesher 18	EAF Su-20	Cannon
19/10/73	113	Hertz Moshe	Nesher	EAF MiG-17	?
19/10/73	113	Hertz Moshe	Nesher	EAF MiG-17	?
19/10/73	113	Yosef Raanan	Nesher 10	EAF MiG-17	Shafrir 2
20/10/73	144	Ben-Nun Assaf	Nesher 34	EAF MiG-21	Shafrir 2
20/10/73	144	Keidar Yermiyahu	Nesher	EAF MiG-21	Shafrir 2
20/10/73	144	Menachem Eliyahu	Nesher	EAF MiG-21	Shafrir 2
20/10/73	101	Epstein Giora	Nesher 61	EAF MiG-21	Cannon
20/10/73	101	Epstein Giora	Nesher 61	EAF MiG-21	Cannon
20/10/73	101	Epstein Giora	Nesher 61	EAF MiG-21	Cannon
20/10/73	101	Epstein Giora	Nesher 61	EAF MiG-21	Shafrir 2

Date	Squadron	Pilot	Aircraft	Kill	Weapon
20/10/73	101	Geva Yoram	Nesher 88	EAF Su-7	AIM-9D
20/10/73	101	Kalichman Amiram	Shahak 89?	EAF Su-7	AIM-9D
20/10/73	113	Aderes Eitan	Nesher	EAF MiG-21	?
20/10/73	144	Lavi Yosef	Nesher	EAF MiG-21	Shafrir 2
20/10/73	144	Yahel Amir	Nesher	EAF MiG-21	Shafrir 2
21/10/73	144	Aven-Nir Uri	Nesher	LARAF Mirage	AAM+cannon
21/10/73	144	Menachem Eliyahu	Nesher	EAF MiG-21	Shafrir 2
21/10/73	144	Keidar Yermiyahu	Nesher	EAF MiG-21	Cannon
21/10/73	144	Keidar Yermiyahu	Nesher	EAF MiG-21	Shafrir 2
21/10/73	101	Geva Yoram	Nesher 88	EAF MiG-21	Cannon
21/10/73	101	Sheffer Yehoshoa	Nesher 76	EAF MiG-21	AIM-9D
21/10/73	113	Gal Yaacov	Nesher	EAF MiG-21	?
21/10/73	113	Hertz Moshe	Nesher	EAF MiG-21	?
21/10/73	113	Levi Shlomo	Nesher 85	EAF MiG-21	Shafrir 2
21/10/73	113	Levi Shlomo	Nesher 85	EAF MiG-21	Shafrir 2
21/10/73	113	Shachar Amos	Nesher	EAF MiG-21	?
21/10/73	117	Liss Uri	Shahak	SAF MiG-21	?
21/10/73	117	Richter Yochai	Shahak	SAF MiG-21	?
21/10/73	117	No 117 Sqn	-	SAF MiG-21	No weapon
21/10/73	117	No 117 Sqn	-	SAF MiG-21	No weapon
22/10/73	101	Haber Michael	Nesher 65	EAF MiG-21 (0.5)	AIM-9D
22/10/73	113	Shachar Amos	Nesher	EAF MiG-21 (0.5)	?
22/10/73	144	No 144 Sqn	-	EAF L-29	No weapon
22/10/73	144	No 144 Sqn	-	EAF L-29	No weapon
22/10/73	101	Karmi Eitan	Shahak 51	SAF MiG-21	Cannon
22/10/73	101	Zuk Michael	Nesher 10	EAF L-29	AIM-9D
22/10/73	113	Levi Shlomo	Nesher 09	SAF MiG-21	Cannon
22/10/73	113	Levi Shlomo	Nesher 09	SAF MiG-21	Shafrir 2
22/10/73	113	Shavit Moshe	Nesher	EAF MiG-21	?
22/10/73	117	Richter Yaacov	Shahak	SAF MiG-21	?
22/10/73	117	Shlaider Daniel	Shahak	SAF MiG-21	?
23/10/73	101	Baharav Israel	Shahak 52	SAF MiG-21	Cannon
23/10/73	101	Kalichman Amiram	Shahak 33	SAF MiG-21	AIM-9D
23/10/73	101	Kalichman Amiram	Shahak 33	SAF MiG-21	AIM-9D
23/10/73	144	Avrahami Michael?	Nesher	EAF MiG-17	Cannon
23/10/73	144	Cohen Ariel	Nesher	EAF MiG-17	Shafrir 2
23/10/73	144	Goren Giora?	Nesher	EAF MiG-17	Shafrir 2
23/10/73	144	No 144 Sqn	-	EAF MiG-17	No weapon
23/10/73	144	Avrahami Michael	Nesher	EAF MiG-21	Cannon
23/10/73	113	Dror Gidon	Nesher	EAF MiG-21	Cannon
23/10/73	113	Gilad Abraham	Nesher	EAF MiG-21	?
23/10/73	113	Gonen Ilan	Nesher	EAF MiG-21	?
23/10/73	117	Richter Yaacov	Shahak	SAF MiG-21	?
23/10/73	117	No 117 Sqn	-	SAF MiG-21	No weapon
24/10/73	144	Erez Shlomo	Nesher	EAF MiG-21	Cannon
24/10/73	144	Menachem Eliyahu	Nesher	EAF MiG-21	Cannon
24/10/73	101	Baharav Israel	Nesher 25	EAF MiG-21	Cannon
24/10/73	101	Baharav Israel	Nesher 25	EAF MiG-21	Cannon
24/10/73	101	Yeari Eliezer	Nesher 11	EAF MiG-21 (0.5)	Shafrir 2
24/10/73	113	Eshchar Amit	Nesher	EAF MiG-21	AAM
24/10/73	113	Gonen Ilan	Nesher	EAF MiG-21	Cannon
24/10/73	113	Gonen Ilan	Nesher	EAF MiG-21	?
24/10/73	113	Gonen Ilan	Nesher	EAF MiG-21	?
24/10/73	101	Epstein Giora	Shahak 86	EAF MiG-21	Cannon
24/10/73	101	Epstein Giora	Shahak 86	EAF MiG-21	AIM-9D
24/10/73	101	Epstein Giora	Shahak 86	EAF MiG-21	AIM-9D
24/10/73	101	Salmon Abraham	Shahak 33	EAF MiG-21	Cannon
24/10/73	101	Sever Dan	Shahak 51	EAF MiG-21 (0.5)	Cannon
24/10/73	101	Zuk Michael	Shahak 89	EAF MiG-21	Cannon
19/4/74	101	Salmon Abraham	Shahak 58	SAF MiG-21	Cannon
19/4/74	101	Salmon Abraham	Shahak 58	SAF MiG-21	AIM-9D
29/4/74	101	Bodinger Hertzel	Nesher 65	SAF MiG-21	AIM-9D
29/4/74	101	Livni Gidon	Nesher 78	SAF MiG-21	Cannon

Key

SAF – Syrian Air Force
EAF – Egyptian Air Force
RJAF – Royal Jordanian Air Force
LAF – Lebanese Air Force
USSR – Soviet Air Force
IrAF – Iraqi Air Force
LARAF – Libyan Arab Republic Air Force

SHAHAK/NESHER LOSSES 1963-1974

Date	Aircraft	Pilot	Notes
24 March 1963	Shahak 6628	Reuven Har'el, ejected	Engine cut
11 September 1963	Shahak 6617	Dan Sever, ejected	Engine explosion
11 November 1963	Shahak 6653	Ran Ronen, ejected	Engine cut, aircraft landed and rebuilt in 1968
11 December 1963	Shahak 6605	Amos Amir, ejected	Engine cut
21 December 1964	Shahak 6627	Michael Barazam, ejected	Fuel starvation, air combat with a Jordanian Hunter
29 June 1965	Shahak 6610	Uri Shachar, ejected	Engine cut
19 October 1965	Shahak 6674	Ilan Hait, ejected	Technical
31 March 1966	Shahak 6672	Yitzhak Barzilai, ejected	Technical
24 August 1966	Shahak 6622	Ya'acov Berman, killed	Training accident
31 January 1967	Shahak 6601	Zur Ben-Barak, killed	Training accident
5 June 1967	Shahak?	Yair Neuman, killed	Air combat with an Egyptian MiG-21
5 June 1967	Shahak 6602	Meir Shachar, killed	AAA, Syria
5 June 1967	Shahak 6616	Amichai Shamueli, ejected	AAA, Syria
5 June 1967	Shahak 6642	Ehud Henkin, ejected	Debris from shot down Syrian MiG-17
7 June 1967	Shahak 6660	Gidon Dror, PoW, Iraq	Air combat with an Iraqi Hunter
7 June 1967	Shahak 6684	David Baruch, killed	SA-2, Egypt
8 June 1967	Shahak 6606	Beni Romach, killed	AAA, Egypt
8 June 1967	Shahak 6609	Maoz Poraz, ejected	Fuel starvation after air combat with Egyptian MiG-21
10 June 1967	Shahak?	Shamuel Sheffer, ejected	AAA, Syria
15 July 1967	Shahak 6620	Shlomo Egozi, ejected	AAA, Egypt, air combat with an Egyptian MiG-21
20 September 1967	Shahak?	Yiz'ar Eshel, killed	Autocommand system malfunction
25 September 1967	Shahak 6626	Yuval Ne'eman, ejected	Engine fire
10 October 1968	Shahak 6655	Shamuel Ben-Rom, injured	Crash landing, aircraft repaired
20 July 1969	Shahak 6656	Eitan Ben-Eliyahu, ejected	AAA, Egypt, air combat with an Egyptian MiG-21
20 July 1969	Shahak?	Eli Zohar, ejected	Air combat with an Egyptian MiG-21
11 September 1969	Shahak 6618	Giora Rom, PoW, Egypt	Air combat with an Egyptian MiG-21
1969/70	Shahak 6645	Avshalom Friedman, ejected	Training accident
2 February 1970	Shahak?	Shlomo Navot, killed	AAA, Syria
9 February 1970	Shahak 6657	Avinoam Keldes, PoW, Egypt	Air combat with an Egyptian MiG-21
2 March 1970	Shahak 6670	Ithamar Neuner, ejected	AAA, Egypt
26 June 1970	Shahak 6631	Boaz Eitan, PoW, Syria	Air combat with a Syrian MiG-21
October 1970	Shahak 6681	Avner Slapak, ejected	?
4 March 1971	Shahak 6655	Yermi Keidar, injured	Engine cut, crash-landing El Arish
1 October 1971	Shahak?	Shaul Keshet, killed	Oscillations
1971/72	?	Avi Lanir, ejected	Collision during DACT
1971/72	?	Ya'acov Gal, ejected	Collision during DACT
9 January 1973	Shahak 6668	Ran Meir, killed	Low flying, crashed into Lake Tiberius
19 February 1973	Nesher 6691	Israel Baharav, ejected	Bird-strike
21 May 1973	Shahak?	Avihu Patishi, ejected	Engine cut
13 September 1973	Shahak?	Yossi Shimchoni, ejected	Air combat with a Syrian MiG-21
7 October 1973	Shahak 6632	Ami Lahav, killed	AAA, Syria
8 October 1973	Nesher 9093	Eitan Karmi, ejected	Air combat with an Egyptian MiG-21
9 October 1973	Shahak 6625	Zvi Vered, PoW, Syria	AAA, Syria
10 October 1973	Nesher 9006	Amos Shachar, ejected	AAA, Egypt
10 October 1973	Shahak 6678	Eitan Karmi, ejected	AAA, Syria
12 October 1973	Shahak 6685	Ami Roke'ach, PoW, Syria	SAM, Syria
13 October 1973	?	Avi Lanir, killed	SAM, Syria
16 October 1973	Nesher 9036	Menachem Kashtan, killed	Air combat with an Egyptian MiG-17
17 October 1973	Shahak 6614	Eliezer Adar, ejected	Fuel starvation after air combat with Syrian MiG-21
20 October 1973	Nesher 9031	Michael Katz, ejected	AAA, Egypt
21 October 1973	Nesher 9076	Yehoshoa Sheffer, ejected	Air combat with an Egyptian MiG-21
6 November 1973	Nesher 9018	Uri Parnas, killed	Training accident
14 December 1973	Nesher?	Nathan Schenk, killed	Training accident
3 February 1974	Nesher 9002	Yitzhak Nir, ejected	Training accident
16 March 1974	Nesher?	Shlomo Levi, ejected	Training accident
6 May 1974	Shahak 6699	Eitan Karmi, ejected	SAM, Syria

COLOUR PLATES

1
Shahak 59 of Yoram Agmon, No 101 Sqn, Hatzor air base, 14 July 1966

The distinction of claiming the first Shahak kill went to Yoram Agmon, who shot down a Syrian MiG-21 while flying Shahak 59 on 14 July 1966. Both pilot and aircraft would subsequently become aces. Agmon flew deltas until 1969, when he converted to the F-4 – he would claim four kills with the Phantom II to add to his two Shahak victories. Pilots flying aircraft 59 scored a total of 13 kills to make it the IDF/AF's most successful Shahak.

2
Shahak 25 of Yehuda Koren, No 117 Sqn, Ramat David air base, 15 August 1966

An ace with 10.5 kills, Koren was credited with his first victory, over a Syrian MiG-21, on 15 August 1966 in Shahak 25. This jet was lost to Syrian AAA on 9 October 1973.

3
Shahak 84 of Ran Ronen, No 119 Sqn, Tel Nof air base, 13 November 1966

Ronen was the first Israeli delta fighter pilot to shoot down a Jordanian Hunter, on 13 November 1966. The Hunter was considered to be an 'inferior' aircraft, yet Ronen's battle with it lasted eight minutes – an eternity by air combat standards.

4
Shahak 34 of Michael Haber, No 101 Sqn, Hatzor air base, 29 November 1966

Haber did not become an ace, adding only half a kill on 22 October 1973 to his initial successes. He did achieve two milestones in Shahak history, however, being the first pilot to down an enemy aircraft using an air-to-air missile, and the first to achieve a double victory – both on 29 November 1966. Shahak 34 was used to shoot down five enemy aircraft.

5
Shahak 52 of Yiftach Spector, No 101 Sqn, Hatzor air base, 7 April 1967

The first shared kill by Shahak pilots was credited to No 101 Sqn's Romach and Spector on 7 April 1967. Romach was later shot down by AAA and killed in the Six Day War, but Spector flew the Shahak until 1971, when he converted to the F-4. Four aces – Baharav, Harish, Livni and Spector – used Shahak 52 to score a combined total of ten kills.

6
Shahak 60 of Avi Lanir, No 117 Sqn, Ramat David air base, 7 April 1967

Even a doomed enemy could still be lethal, with at least one Shahak being lost after it was hit by debris when its victim exploded. There were also many cases of delta fighters returning to base covered in oil, including Avi Lanir, who flew through the explosion of his victim's MiG-21 on 7 April 1967. Barely able to see, he was escorted back to Ramat David by No 119 Sqn senior deputy CO Moti Yeshurun. Shahak 60 was lost over Iraq two months later.

7
Shahak 77 of Dan Sever, No 101 Sqn, Hatzor air base, 5 June 1967

The first 'no weapon' kill was credited to Sever on 5 June 1967. Initially, when enemy aircraft crashed without a shot being fired, the loss was awarded to the pilots involved, but later they were considered to be 'squadron kills'. Two such victories were credited to Shahak 77 out of a total of 23.

8
Shahak 06 of Baruch Friedman, No 101 Sqn, Hatzor air base, 6 June 1967

During the Six Day War, 13 pilots shared the 14 kills credited to No 101 Sqn, with the final one being considered a squadron victory. Both Baruch Friedman and Shahak 06 were credited with a single Egyptian Su-7 kill, on 6 June 1967.

9
Shahak 45 of Yehuda Koren, No 117 Sqn, Ramat David air base, 6 June 1967

This aircraft wears what were possibly the most extraordinary kill markings displayed by any Shahak. Aven-Nir shot down a Lebanese Hunter in this aircraft on 5 June 1967, and 24 hours later Koren claimed an Iraqi Hunter and a MiG-21.

10
Shahak 56 of Giora Epstein, No 101 Sqn, Hatzor air base, 6 June 1967

The leading Israeli ace, Epstein scored the first (an Egyptian Su-7) of his 17 kills while flying Shahak 56 on 6 June 1967. The aircraft was used to score four kills before it was lost in July 1969 (to AAA), and until then 56 was perhaps the unit's most valuable fighter. Yiftach Spector later wrote a song in its honour, while Giora Epstein duly called it 'the best aircraft we had – better than 59 and better than 82. Simply the best'.

11
Shahak 09 of Amos Amir, No 101 Sqn, Hatzor air base, 7 June 1967

Amir flew the Shahak until 1970, firstly with No 101 Sqn and from 1968 as CO of No 119 Sqn. His Egyptian MiG-19 kill on 7 June 1967 was both his and Shahak 09's first victory. It would prove to be the jet's only score.

12
Shahak 29 of Ezra Dotan, No 117 Sqn, Ramat David air base, 7 June 1967

During the afternoon of 7 June 1967, Ezra 'Baban' Dotan, in Shahak 29 and David Porat, in Shahk 76, flew to Iraq in an attempt to locate distress radio signals from four aircrewmen lost that morning over H-3. It was to be an eventful mission for Dotan, as Porat later reported. 'We saw nothing, so we strafed once, cleared the area and pulled up. Returning at high altitude, near Lake Tiberius I noticed small puffs of smoke close to "Baban". I warned him and then saw an AAM. I yelled, "Break!" but "Baban" was hit, and I then saw two MiG-21s. It was a ground control error. They thought that we and the MiG-21s were a four-ship formation of Syrian fighters, so they had vectored a pair of Shahaks, led by Yehuda Koren, to intercept us. Koren arrived and told me to "Go home. I'm in charge". "Baban" landed his badly damaged aircraft at Megiddo'.

13
Shahak 41 of Giora Rom, No 119 Sqn, Tel Nof air base, 7 June 1967

Rom became the first Israeli ace over the course of just three days in June 1967. His last two kills (Egyptian MiG-17s) were claimed while flying Shahak 41 on 7 June 1967. Rom retired from IDF/AF service in 1996 with the rank of major general.

14
Shahak 15 of Yossi Arazi, No 101 Sqn, Hatzor air base, 8 June 1967

Arazi flew with No 101 Sqn between 1965 and 1967, during which time he took part in two aerial combats and scored a single kill. Shahak 15 was used to score four victories between 1967 and 1970.

15
Shahak 68 of Avraham Salmon, No 119 Sqn, Tel Nof air base, 8 June 1967

Shahak 68 was credited with 11 kills in No 119 Sqn service between 1967 and 1970, including four claimed by Avraham Salmon. In fact Salmon was the first to down an aircraft while flying this jet, scoring a double kill on 8 June 1967.

16
Shahak 14 of Michael Zuk, No 101 Sqn, Hatzor air base, 8 March 1969

Both Zuk and Shahak 14 were credited with their first victory on the first day of the Attrition War. A seven-kill ace, Zuk died in a Kfir crash in 1975, while No 14 was lost to fuel starvation following combat with a Syrian MiG-21 on 17 October 1973.

17
Shahak 58 of Reuven Rozen, No 119 Sqn, Tel Nof air base, 21 May 1969

Rozen flew delta fighters between 1966 and 1983. His first two kills, scored on 8 June 1967 and 21 May 1969, were in fact the first two credited to Shahak 58.

18
Shahak 19 of Amos Amir, No 119 Sqn, Tel Nof air base, 24 June 1969

Operation *Rimonim*, which was supposed to deter Egyptian aggression with an Israeli show of force in the War of Attrition, commenced when No 119 Sqn CO Amir downed an Egyptian MiG-21 flying the unit's flagship, Shahak 19.

19
Shahak 33 of Eitan Ben-Eliyahu, No 101 Sqn, Hatzor air base, 8 July 1969

Commander of the IDF/AF between 1996 and 2000, Ben-Eliyahu achieved his first kill flying Shahak 33 on 8 July 1969. His next two victories were claimed with the F-4, and his fourth, and final, kill came in an F-15. Pilots flying Shahak 33 scored a combined total of six kills between 1967 and 1973, Ben-Eliyahu's being the jet's third victory.

20
Shahak 82 of Israel Baharav, No 101 Sqn, Hatzor air base, 6 October 1969

Although a pleasant character on the ground, Baharav was one of the most aggressive delta fighter pilots. All 12 of his kills were MiG-21s, and they were claimed in just seven engagements, including five double victories. Baharav was flying Shahak 82 when he scored his first two kills, which were the fourth and fifth enemy aircraft to fall to this jet. Shahak 82 would become No 101 Sqn's most popular aircraft.

21
Shahak 79 of Yitzhak Nir, No 119 Sqn, Tel Nof air base, 28 April 1970

An engagement with Su-7s in which he claimed his first kill inspired Yitzhak Nir to produce a painting called 'The Hit', which depicted the Egyptian jet's last moments. Shahak 79 served with No 119 Sqn until 1970, when it was sent to No 117. Here, it scored more kills than with its previous unit.

22
Shahak 80 of Reuven Rozen, No 119 Sqn, Tel Nof air base, 14 May 1970

Rozen became the first Shahak pilot to down an enemy aircraft using the AIM-9B AAM in April 1969. He also claimed the fourth kill with the new weapon, on 14 May 1970. That year saw 38 per cent of all Shahak kills scored by AAMs.

23
Shahak 64 of Yehuda Koren, No 117 Sqn, Ramat David air base, 15 May 1970

Yehuda Koren became an ace on 15 May 1970 in an action which he later described as follows. 'The controller joined us with a No 119 Sqn pair led by Salmon. When we turned south I became leader, and there was a MiG-21 which I don't think had seen me. We were deep into Egypt, near Inchas and Bilbeis. I launched from quite a distance – maybe 2000 m. Usually when you launched at a proper range, the rocket still burned when the missile hit the aircraft. In this case it flamed-out, and I thought I'd missed, but then came the explosion'.

24
Shahak 15 of Moshe Hertz, No 101 Sqn, Hatzor air base, 10 July 1970

Hertz scored his first, and only, kill during his time with No 101 Sqn in this jet, but it was the fourth, and final, one to be claimed by a pilot flying Shahak 15. As the No 113 Sqn senior deputy CO, Hertz was credited with 5.5 kills in October 1973.

25
Shahak 78 of Avraham Salmon, No 119 Sqn, Tel Nof air base, 30 July 1970

Salmon used Shahak 78 to become the first Israeli pilot to down a Soviet-flown fighter. Following its transfer to No 101 Sqn, Shahak 78 claimed four more kills between September 1972 and September 1973. It was downed by Syrian AAA on 10 October 1973.

26
Nesher 15 of Assaf Ben-Nun, No 144 Sqn, Etszion air base, 6 October 1973

Assaf Ben-Nun was a highly experienced pilot, having served in the 1956 and 1967 campaigns. He scored his first kill while flying the Mystere, and was later a test pilot with Israeli Aircraft Industries, becoming Kfir project chief test pilot. Appropriately, he was the first Nesher pilot to shoot down an enemy aircraft, on 6 October 1973. His leader in that combat, Yermi Keidar, could also boast long experience, as he had been credited with his first kill while flying the Super Mystere.

27
Shahak 59 of Eitan Karmi, No 101 Sqn, Hatzor air base, 6 October 1973

Karmi achieved a unique kill when he shot down an AS-5 ASM launched by an Egyptian Tu-16 bomber on 6 October 1973. Shahak 59 was damaged in an accident at Hatzor the following day, injuring its pilot, Israel Baharav (squadron senior deputy CO). The latter returned to flying status as acting CO after the loss of Lanir on 13 October.

28
Nesher 28 of Menachem Sharon, No 144 Sqn, Etszion air base, 8 October 1973

Sharon commanded No 144 Sqn in 1973-74, flying 56 sorties during the Yom Kippur War. On 8 October 1973, he and his wingman, Shimcha Kelman, intercepted four Egyptian MiG-17s on their way to attack the SAM Hawk battery at Gidi Pass. The Nesher pilots downed the trailing pair of MiG-17s using Shafrir 2 AAMs, before switching to the leading pair. Kelman repeated this feat, but Sharon was too close when he launched his second Shafrir 2, and the AAM failed to hit. The MiG-17 pilot was able to return home to tell of his escape.

29
Shahak 52 of Dror Harish, No 101 Sqn, Hatzor air base, 9 October 1973

Harish became an ace when he destroyed two MiG-17s in Shahak 52 on 9 October 1973. Other pilots had already claimed six victories with the jet prior to this combat.

30
Shahak 07 of Yehuda Koren, No 117 Sqn, Ramat David air base, 10 October 1973

The Yom Kippur War was in its fourth day when Yehuda Koren used this aircraft to down a Syrian MiG-17. Zvika Vered had also enjoyed success with it three days earlier, claiming a MiG-21 kill despite having no afterburner or AAMs due to a technical malfunction. He downed his MiG with cannon fire.

31
Nesher 21 of Shlomo Levi, No 113 Sqn, Hatzor air base, 12 October 1973

Shlomo Levi was the second highest scoring delta pilot of the Yom Kippur War with ten kills, including three Syrian Su-7s downed on 12 October 1973. Flying Nesher 21, his wingman on the mission was Hatzor base CO Amos Lapidot, who he was leading on a CAP over the Golan Heights.

32
Nesher 33 of Assaf Ben-Nun, No 144 Sqn, Etszion air base, 14 October 1973

IAI test pilot Ben-Nunn was flying Nesher 33 on 14 October 1973 when he encountered a MiG-21. During the subsequent battle, the MiG exploded under the impact of his cannon fire. Ben-Nunn flew through the debris and his engine cut, so he drew on his experience as a test pilot to methodically run through the procedures needed to re-start the fighter in flight. He soon had the engine running again.

33
Nesher 61 of Giora Epstein, No 113 Sqn, Hatzor air base, 20 October 1973

Although a No 101 Sqn pilot, Epstein downed eight aircraft while flying No 113 Sqn's Nesher 61. After the war, there was a debate about the best way of attributing kills between the two Hatzor-based units who had shared aircraft. The matter was resolved by crediting them to the pilot concerned, so that when No 101 Sqn pilot Karmi claimed two kills flying No 113's Nesher 93 on 10 October, but was then shot down, the kills were attributed to No 101 and the loss to No 113!

34
Shahak 58 of Avraham Salmon, No 101 Sqn, Hatzor air base, 19 April 1974

The last Shahak double kill was credited to Salmon in No 58.

35
Shahak 103, Eitham air base, 1981

A few Shahaks were repainted in air superiority grey in the twilight of their operational careers, including No 103, which also displayed eight kill markings.

36
Shahak 111, Eitham air base, 1981

Shahak 11 was damaged in a take-off accident in October 1969, repaired with Nesher wings and is now on display at the IDF/AF Museum.

37
Shahak 153, Eitham air base, 1981

Although Shahak 53 crashed (whilst being flown by future ace Ran Ronen) in November 1963, it was subsequently repaired and returned to active service in 1968.

38
Shahak 107, Eitham air base, 1981

Although not flown by one of the IDF/AF's top aces, Shahak 07 nevertheless provided good service between 1962 and 1982. All surviving Shahaks flew from Eitham in their final years of active service.

39
Nesher 666, Flight Test Centre, Tel Nof, late 1970s

Ten two-seat Neshers were produced by IAI and delivered to the IDF/AF in 1974-75.

Back cover
Nesher 16 of Yoram Geva, No 101 Sqn, Hatzor air base, 8 January 1973

The distinction of claiming the first Nesher kill went to Yoram Geva, who shot down a Syrian MiG-21 with an AIM-9D while flying this aircraft on 8 January 1973. Geva went on to score another three kills in October 1973 to become an ace.

COLOUR SECTION

1
Top Israeli ace Giora Epstein scored 12 kills in five air combats during the Yom Kippur War. He claimed his kills in three aircraft – eight in Nesher 61, three in Shahak 86 and a single one in Shahak 11. Epstein used cannon fire to down seven of his kills, two fell to AIM-9Ds and the remaining three to the Shafrir 2. Dressed in casual attire – an Epstein trademark – the ace stands by 'his' Nesher 61 (*via Peter Mersky*)

2
Shahaks and Neshers were treated like kings when in frontline service, and they deserved to be

3
No 101 Sqn CO Oded Marom achieved ace status on 4 January 1970. He was only the fourth Israeli pilot to reach this milestone (*via Peter Mersky*)

4
Top ace Shahak 59 is seen in flight shortly before it was sold to Argentina in the wake of the 1982 Falklands War. Having spent its last years in South America on ignominious display in front of a regional school, this important fighter recently returned to Israel for display in the IDF/AF Museum (*via Peter Mersky*)

BIBLIOGRAPHY

MAGAZINES

Aloni, Shlomo, 'Israeli Ace – The Combat Career of Ran Ronen', *FlyPast* issue 188, p74-78, March 1997

Aloni, Shlomo, 'Shahaks over the Desert', *Wings of Fame* Volume 16, p138-147 and Volume 17 p16-25, 1999

Aloni, Shlomo, 'Suez Combat', *Air Forces Monthly* issue 139 p52-57, October 1999

Aloni, Shlomo, 'Shafrir 2', *Air Forces Monthly* issue 151 p70-72, October 2000

Nordeen, Lon, 'Air Warfare in the Middle East', *Air Forces Monthly* issues 133 p46-50 & 134 p30-34, April and May 1999

BOOKS

Aloni, Shlomo, *Arab-Israeli Air Wars, 1947-1982*, Osprey Publishing, 2001

Borovik, Yehuda, *Israeli Air Force, Warbirds Illustrated*, No 23, Arms and Armour Press, 1984

Cohen, Eliezer, *Israel's Best Defence*, Airlife, 1993

Dor, Amos, *The IAF Series No 3/1 – The Mirage IIIC Shahak*, AD Graphica, 1999

Gunston, Bill, *An Illustrated Guide to the Israeli Air Force*, Salamander Books, 1982

Lapidot, Aharon and Merav Halperin, *G-Suit*, Sphere Books, 1990

Mafe, Salvador, *Dassault-Breguet Mirage III/5*, Osprey, 1990

Mersky, Peter B, *Israeli Fighter Aces*, Speciality Press, 1997

Nordeen, Lon, *Fighters over Israel*, Orion Books, 1990

Nordeen, Lon and David Nicolle, *Phoenix Over the Nile*, Smithsonian Institution Press, 1997

Weizman, Ezer, *On Eagle's Wings*, Weidenfeld and Nicholson, 1976

Yonai, Ehud, *No Margin for Error*, Pantheon Press, 1993

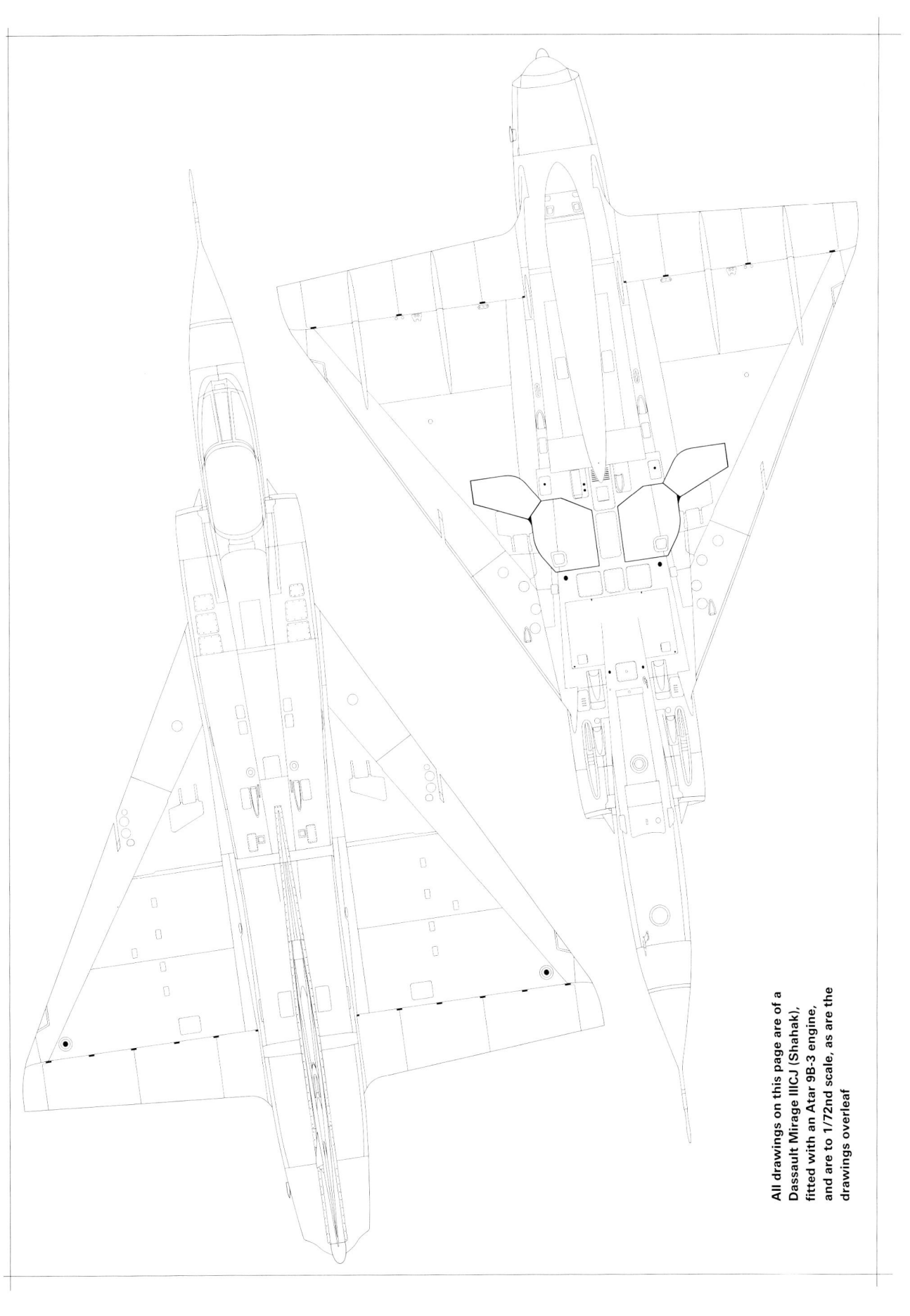

All drawings on this page are of a Dassault Mirage IIICJ (Shahak), fitted with an Atar 9B-3 engine, and are to 1/72nd scale, as are the drawings overleaf

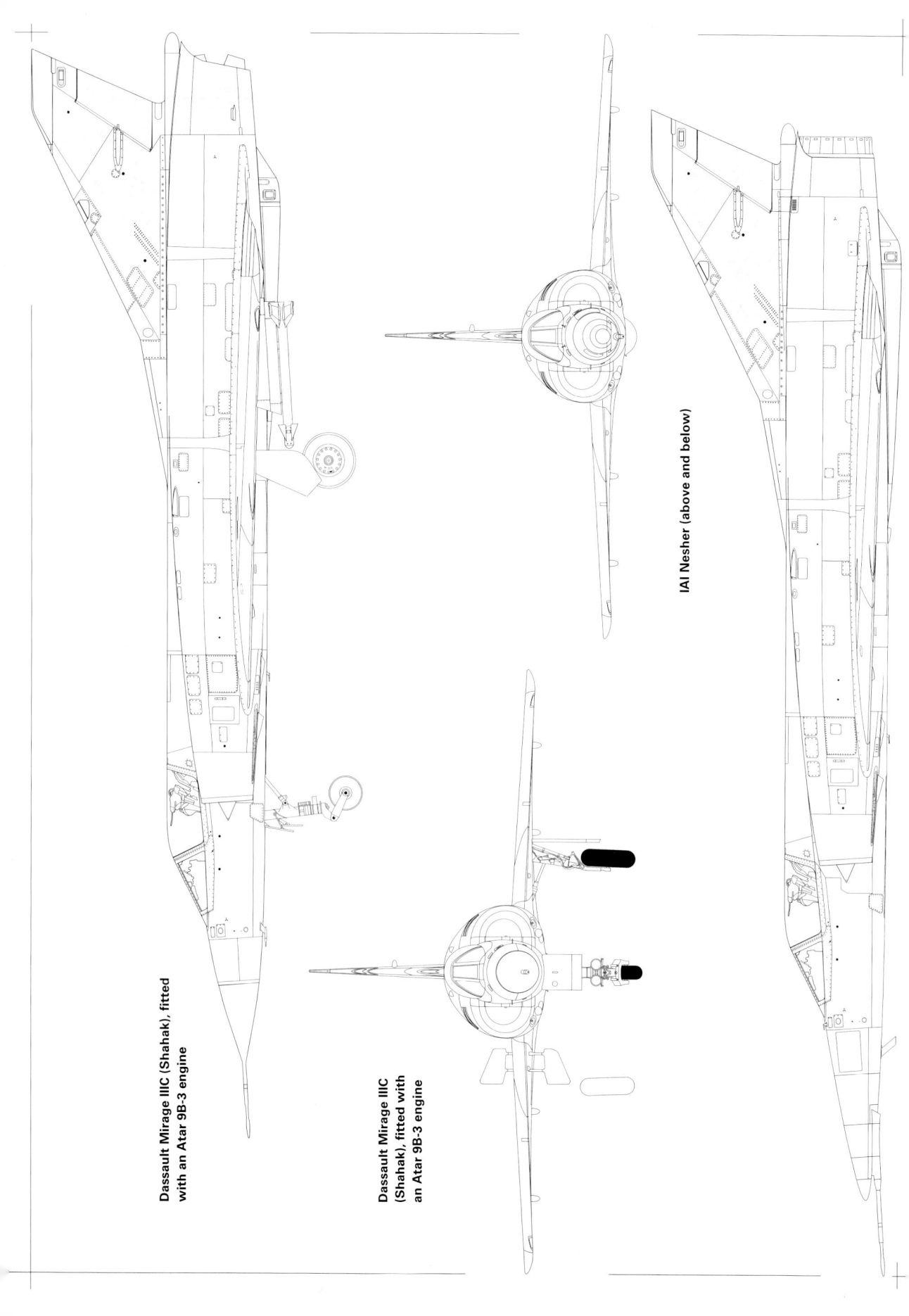

Dassault Mirage IIIC (Shahak), fitted with an Atar 9B-3 engine

Dassault Mirage IIIC (Shahak), fitted with an Atar 9B-3 engine

IAI Nesher (above and below)

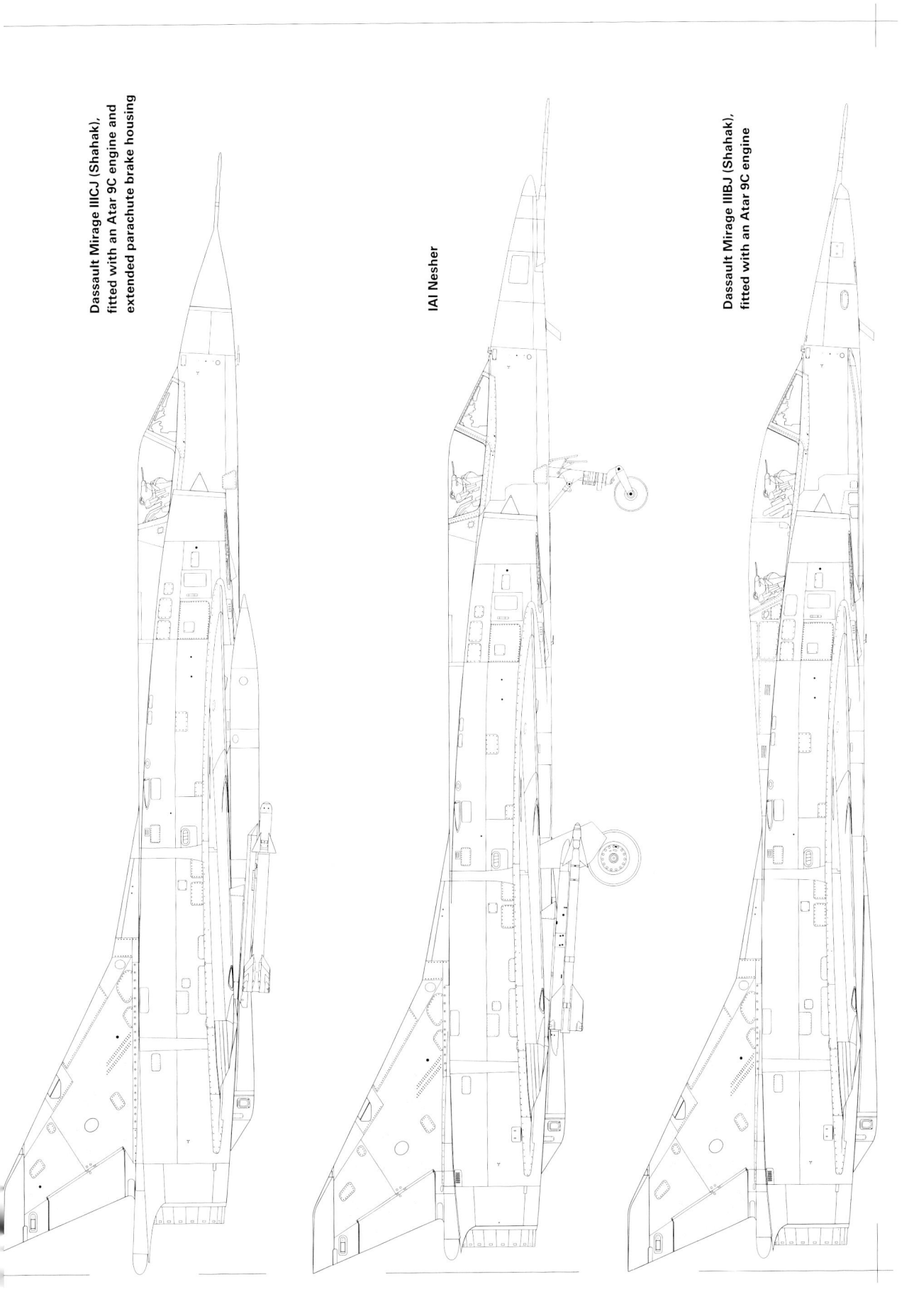

Dassault Mirage IIICJ (Shahak), fitted with an Atar 9C engine and extended parachute brake housing

IAI Nesher

Dassault Mirage IIIBJ (Shahak), fitted with an Atar 9C engine

INDEX

References to illustrations are shown in **bold**. Colour Plates are prefixed 'pl.' and Colour Section illustrations 'cs.', with page and caption locators in (brackets).

Afek, Omri **14**, 38, **50**
Agassi, Ya'acov 43, 70-71
Agmon, Yoram 12, **13**, 13, pl.**1**(17, 89), **42**, 45
Aharon, Ezra 14-15, **15**, **42**
Al-Minya air base **36**
alert complex **14**, **33**, **34**, **45**, 45, **46**
Amir, Amos **9**, **10**, pl.**11**(20, 89), 39, **40**, **58**, 58, 59, 60, 62
   Attrition War pl.**18**(22, 90), 49-50, 52, 55
Arad, Amnon 36, 37, **39**, **43**
Arazi, Yossi **13**, pl.**14**(21, 90), 40-42, **41**, **42**
Ardaka air base 35
Ashkenazi, Efraim **10**, 11, 12
Attrition War 46-56
Augarten, Rudy 39-40
Aven-Nir, Uri **14**, 36, **37**, **43**, 50, 55, 56, 63, **64**
Avrahami, Mikey **64**

Baharav, Israel pl.**20**(23, 90), 48, **54**, **55**, **56**, **58**, **61**, 61-62, **77**, 77, 91
Barzilai, Yitzhak **10**, 36, **42**
Ben-Eliyahu, Eitan pl.**19**(23, 90), **50**, 50, **54**, 80
Ben-Nun, Assaf pl.**26**(25, 90-91), pl.**32**(27, 91), 64-65, **67**, 67-68, 79
Ben-Nun, Avihu 44-45, **46**, **50**
Ben-Or, Aryeh 41, 42
Berman, Ya'acov **12**

Cairo West air base **33**, 39
Cohen, Ariel 75-76
Convair F-106 Delta Dart 6

Dassault
   Mirage III 6-7, **7**, **8** see also Dassault Shahak
   Mirage IIIA03: **6**
   Mirage IIIB: 6
   Mirage IIIBJ **8**, **46**
   Mirage IIIC 6
   Mirage IIICJ **8**
   Shahak (Skyblazer) 8, **10**, 13, **14**, 15, **33**, **39**, **60**, 62, **80**, 80
      cockpit **12**
      gunsight, CSF-95: 10, 11-12, **12** see also gunsight cameras
      radar, CSF Cyrano **9**, 10, **12**, 12
      weapons system 9-12
   Shahak 02: **16**
   Shahak 03: 56, **63**
   Shahak 06: pl.**8**(19, 89)
   Shahak 07: pl.**30**(26, 91), **68**
   Shahak 09: **16**, pl.**11**(20, 89), **40**
   Shahak 11: **56**
   Shahak 12: 46
   Shahak 14: pl.**16**(22, 90), **47**
   Shahak 15: pl.**14**(21, 90), pl.**24**(24, 90), **41**
   Shahak 19 pl.**18**(22, 90), 51-52, **63**, **74**
   Shahak 22: **12**
   Shahak 25 pl.**2**(17, 89)
   Shahak 29 pl.**12**(20, 89-90), **40**
   Shahak 32: 55, **63**
   Shahak 33 pl.**19**(23, 90), **50**
   Shahak 34 pl.**4**(18, 89)
   Shahak 41 pl.**13**(21, 90), **63**
   Shahak 42: **16**
   Shahak 45 pl.**9**(19, 89), **37**
   Shahak 50: **71**
   Shahak 51: **16**, **69**
   Shahak 52-11, **16**, pl.**5**(18, 89), pl.**29**(26, 91), **70**
   Shahak 53: **8**, **51**
   Shahak 55: 42, 43, 55-56, 66
   Shahak 56 pl.**10**(20, 89), **37**
   Shahak 58 pl.**17**(22, 90), pl.**34**(28, 91), 42, **63**, **79**, 79
   Shahak 59: **13**, pl.**1**(17, 89), pl.**27**(25, 91), pl.**4**(32, 92), **35**, 51, 56, **59**, **61**, **77**
   Shahak 60: **16**, pl.**6**(18, 89)
   Shahak 64 pl.**23**(24, 90), **43**, 64-65
   Shahak 66: **57**, **63**
   Shahak 68 pl.**15**(21, 90), 56, **63**
   Shahak 77 pl.**7**(19, 89), **34**
   Shahak 78 pl.**25**(25, 90), **62**, **63**
   Shahak 79 pl.**21**(23, 90), **59**, **63**, **65**
   Shahak 80 pl.**22**(24, 90), **52**, **58**, **63**
   Shahak 82 pl.**20**(23, 90), 56
   Shahak 83: **45**, **52**, **63**
   Shahak 84: **15**, 15, pl.**3**(17, 89)
   Shahak 85: **63**
   Shahak 89: **46**, **63**
   Shahak 98 and 99: **63**
   Shahak 103 pl.**35**(28, 91)
   Shahak 107 pl.**38**(29, 91)
   Shahak 111 pl.**36**(28, 91)
   Shahak 153 pl.**37**(29, 91)

Dotan, Ezra 'Baban' **14**, 15, **16**, pl.**12**(20, 89-90), 36, **39**, 39, **40**, 40, **43**
Dror, Gidon **4**, **10**, **12**, **14**, **39**, 39, **63**, **70**, **76**, 76-77

Egyptian Air Defence Force (ADF) 44
Egyptian Third Army 73, 76
English Electric Lightning 6
Epstein, Giora pl.**33**(27, 91), cs.**1**(32, 92), 51, 52-53, **54**, 58, **63**, 76, 78, 79, **80**
   Six-Day War pl.**10**(20, 89), 36, **37**, **42**
Eshchar, Amit **74**, **76**
Eyal, Menachem 47, 48, 52

Fayid air base **35**
Friedman, Avshalom 54, **55**, 56, 69
Friedman, Baruch pl.**8**(19, 89), 36, 39
fuel tanks, supersonic **7**, **11**, **61**, **69**, 69-70
Furman, Giora 38, **42**, 50

Geva, Yoram **63**, **64**, 91
Gil, Uri 36, **43**
Gilad, Avi **55**, 58, 62, **70**
Gonen, Ilan **13**, 34, **35**, **70**, 70
Goren, Giora **54**
gunsight cameras **9**, **13**, **15**, **16**, **35**, **65**, **71**, **75**, 76

H-3 air base, Iraq 36, 37-39, **39**
Haber, Michael 'Diamond' 15, pl.**4**(18, 89), **42**, **63**
Hait, Ilan **13**, 43, **50**
Har'el, Reuven **14**, **39**, 39, **43**
Harish, Dror **4**, pl.**29**(26, 91), 59, **70**, 70
Harlev, Rafi 48, 49
Hassan, Muhamad Abed El-Baki Ahmed 47
Hawker Hunter 8, 9, 10, **15**, 15, 89
Henkin, Ehud **13**, 36, **43**, 43, 55
Henkin, Yossi **43**, 51
Hertz, Moshe **4**, pl.**24**(24, 90), **63**, **76**
Hod, Maj Gen Moti 52, **57**

IAI (Israeli Aircraft Industries)
   Nesher (Eagle) 63-65, 68, **79**, 80
      cockpit **64**
      gunsight **70** see also gunsight cameras
   Nesher 09: **4**, **75**
   Nesher 10: **4**, **75**
   Nesher 15 pl.**26**(25, 90-91), **67**
   Nesher 16: **64**, 91
   Nesher 18: **74**
   Nesher 21 pl.**31**(27, 91), **72**
   Nesher 23: **69**
   Nesher 25: **77**
   Nesher 28 pl.**28**(26, 91)
   Nesher 33 pl.**32**(27, 91)
   Nesher 61 pl.**33**(27, 91), cs.**1**(32, 92)
   Nesher 78: **79**, 79
   Nesher 666 pl.**39**(29, 91)
Ilyushin Il-14: **35**
Ilyushin Il-28: **33**, **35**
Israeli Defence Force/Air Force (IDF/AF)
   aircrew categories 12
   courses **10**, **13**, **14**, **55**
   Flight Test Centre pl.**39**(29, 91)
   No 101 Sqn **7**, 8, **10**, **11**, **12**, **16**, pl.**1**(17, 89), pl.**4**, **5**(18, 89), pl.**34**(28, 91), 45, **79**, **91**
      Attrition War pl.**16**(22, 90), pl.**19**, **20**(23, 90), pl.**24**(24, 90), 48, **51**, 51
      pilots **43**
      Six-Day War pl.**7**, **8**(19, 89), pl.**10**, **11**(20, 89), pl.**14**(21, 90), 38, 39
      Yom Kippur War **4**, pl.**27**(25, 91), pl.**29**(26, 91), **69**, 69, **77**
   No 113 Sqn **4**, pl.**31**, **33**(27, 91), 65, **69**, 69
      pilots **76**
   No 117 Sqn **7**, 8, **12**, **16**, pl.**2**(17, 89), pl.**6**(18, 89), pl.**30**(26, 91), 69, **71**
      Attrition War pl.**23**(24, 90), 49, 51, 55
      pilots **43**
      Six-Day War pl.**9**(19, 89), pl.**12**(20, 89-90), 36, 38, **39**
   No 119 Sqn **13**, **14**, pl.**3**(17, 89), **58**, 63, **63**
      Attrition War pl.**17**, **18**(22, 90), pl.**21**(23, 90), pl.**22**(24, 90), pl.**25**(25, 90), 48, 55
      pilots **50**, **58**
      Six-Day War pl.**13**, **15**(21, 90), 35, 36, 38
   No 144 Sqn pl.**26**(25, 90-91), pl.**28**(26, 91), pl.**32**(27, 91), **64**, 65, 66, 69
   'Shahak Zeroing Team' 11
Ivry, David 34

Karmi, Eitan pl.**27**(25, 91), 35, 49-50, **50**, **63**
Keidar, Yermi **64**, 66-68, 91
Keldes, Avinoam 49
kills 16, 34-35, 43, 50, 51, **78**, 79, 80, 89
Koren, Yehuda **14**, 14, pl.**17**(22, 90), pl.**23**(24, 90), pl.**30**(26, 91), 52-53, 60-61, 63, 90
   Six-Day War pl.**9**(19, 89), 36, **37**, 37-38, **39**, 40, **43**

Lanir, Avi **14**, 15, **16**, pl.**6**(18, 89), **43**, 66, 70

Lapidot, Amos **42**, 52, 53, 72, **76**, 91
Lev, Arlozor **10**, 40, **42**
Levi, Shlomo pl.**31**(27, 91), **54**, **55**, **72**, 72-75, **74**, **76**, 77
Levoshin, Arnon **14**, 35, **50**
Liss, Uri **14**, **43**, 46
Livni, Gidon **4**, **75**, **77**, **79**, 79-80
Lockheed F-104 Starfighter 6
low-level flight profiles **9**

markings, squadron and kill **30-31**, cs.**1-3**(32, 92), **66**
Marom, Oded **11**, cs.**3**(32, 92), **38**, 38, 46, 49, **54**, 57
McDonnell Douglas F-4 Phantom II 54, 57
Meir, Ran **55**, 65
Menachem, Eli 49, **64**, 76, 78
Mikoyan
   MiG-17: **4**, 8, 9, 10, **36**, 40, 42, **55**, 55, **70**
   MiG-19: **40**
   MiG-21: **4**, 6, 8, **9**, **13**, 13, **14**, 14-15, **16**, **34**, **41**, 41, **75**, **76**, **78**, 79

Nasser, President Abdel Gamal El 44, 52, 57
Navot, Shlomo **14**, **43**, 50, 51, 54, 55, 57
Ne'eman, Yuval **14**, **43**, 54-55, **65**, 65, 75
Neuner, Ithamar 38, 49, 63, 70, **78**
Nir, Yitzhak pl.**21**(23, 90), **50**, 51-53, 55-56, **58**, 58-59, **59**

Operation *Boxer* 51-53
Operation *Pricha* (Blossom) 57-59
Operation *Rimonim* (Pomegranates) 49-50, 90
Operation *Zola 1 to 15*: **8**

Peled, Maj Gen Beni **42**, 66, 71, 72, **76**
Peri, Elisha 69, **71**, **78**
Pessach, Shraga **14**, 36, **39**, **43**
Piada, Ya'acov **64**
Porat, David **13**, **39**, 39, **43**
Poraz, Maoz 40, 41, 42
Prigat, Eliezer 45

Rabin, Lt Gen Yitzhak **37**
Ran, Avshalom **11**, 36
Redifim air base **4**, **45**, 45, **46**, **47**, 47, 68
Richter, Kobi **9**, 46, 50, 60, 63, 77
Roke'ach, Amichai **14**, **43**, 71
Rom, Giora **13**, pl.**13**(21, 90), 35, 36, 39, 40, 43, 52, 56
Ronen, Ran **8**, **11**, **15**, 15, pl.**3**(17, 89), **44**, 44-45, **48**, **50**
   Attrition War 48, 49, 56
   Six-Day War 35, 36, 40
Rozen, Reuven pl.**17**(22, 90), pl.**22**(24, 90), 42-43, 47-48, 49, **50**, **58**, 59-60, **63**, 70, 71-72

Saab 35 Draken 6
Sa'ar, Moshe 'Simi' 38
Sagi, Oded 13, 35, 36, 38, 40
Salmon, Avraham **4**, **10**, pl.**15**(21, 90), pl.**25**(25, 90), pl.**34**(28, 91), 40, 42, 58, **70**, 79, 79
   Attrition War **58**, **62**, 62
Sever, Dan **11**, 13, pl.**7**(19, 89), 33-34, **34**, **42**, 45, **46**, **63**, **78**, 79
Shachar, Uri 38, 39
Shamir, Amnon **42**, 46
Shamueli, Amichai 'Shumi' **14**, **43**, 52
Shapira, Danny **6**, **8**, **14**, **46**
Sharon, Menachem pl.**28**(26, 91), 54, **60**, 61, 66, **73**, 73
Shmul, Menachem 40, 43, 56, 67, 68
Slapak, Avner **10**, 13, 15-16, 41, **42**, 80
Snir, Asher 36, 43, 45, **47**, 49-50, **50**, 58, 59, 62, 77
   Attrition War 49-50, 56, **58**
Spector, Yiftach 15, pl.**5**(18, 89), **42**, 49, 51, 61, **63**, 63, 77-78
Sukhoi Su-7: 9, 10, **35**

training 10-11, **11**, 14, 55, 65
Tupolev Tu-16: **33**

Vered, Zvika **65**, 66, **68**, 69, 70, 91

weapons
   bombs, 500-kg 8
   cannon, DEFA 552 30 mm 8, 10, 13, **59**
   missiles
      AA-2 Atoll air-to-air (AAM) **47**, 47
      AIM-9B Sidewinder infra-red (IR) AAM 47, **50**, 90
      AIM-9D AAM 47, **50**, **60**
      AS-1 air-to-surface **33**
      R.530 Yahalom SARH AAM **7**, **11**, 15, **61**
      Rafael Shafrir (Dragonfly) IR AAM 15, 43, **44**, 45
      Shafrir 2 IR AAM 47, 49, 50, **60**, **64**
Weizman, Maj Gen Ezer **6**, **7**, **80**

Ye'ari, Uri 38, **50**, 55
Yeshurun, Moti **11**, 89
Yoeli, Giora 47, 51
Yosef, Ra'anan **4**, 70, **76**, 79

Zuk, Michael pl.**16**(22, 90), **47**, 47, 51, **63**, 75
Zur, Ran 38